Attracting and Feeding Backyard Birds

CAROL FRISCHMANN

Attracting and Feeding Backyard Birds

Project Team
Editor: Tom Mazorlig
Copy Editor: Joann Woy
Interior Design: Leah Lococo Ltd. and Stephanie Krautheim
Design Layout: Patricia Escabi

T.F.H. Publications
President/CEO: Glen S. Axelrod
Executive Vice President: Mark E. Johnson
Publisher: Christopher T. Reggio
Production Manager: Kathy Bontz

T.F.H. Publications, Inc.
One TFH Plaza
Third and Union Avenues
Neptune City, NJ 07753

Discovery Communications, Inc. Book Development Team
Marjorie Kaplan, President, Animal Planet Media
Carol LeBlanc, Vice President, Licensing
Elizabeth Bakacs, Vice President, Creative Services
Brigid Ferraro, Director, Licensing
Peggy Ang, Vice President, Animal Planet Marketing
Caitlin Erb, Licensing Specialist

Printed and bound in China
07 08 09 10 11 1 3 5 7 9 8 6 4 2

Library of Congress Cataloging-in-Publication Data
Frischmann, Carol.
  Attracting and feeding backyard birds / Carol Frischmann.
    p. cm. — (Animal planet pet care library)
  ISBN 978-0-7938-3786-1 (alk. paper)
 1. Bird attracting. 2. Birds—Feeding and feeds. 3. Birds. I. Title.
QL676.5.F77 2007
639.9'78—dc22
                    2007014222

This book has been published with the intent to provide accurate and authoritative information in regard to the subject matter within. While every precaution has been taken in preparation of this book, the author and publisher expressly disclaim responsibility for any errors, omissions, or adverse effects arising from the use or application of the information contained herein. The techniques and suggestions are used at the reader's discretion and are not to be considered a substitute for veterinary care. If you suspect a medical problem consult your veterinarian.

The Leader In Responsible Animal Care For Over 50 Years!®
www.tfh.com

CENTRAL
Garden & Pet

Table of Contents

Chapter 1

Who Are Your

Backyard Birds?

Birds in the backyard, whether your yard is a farm or a window, add beauty, mystery, and drama to each day. Unlike a pet, backyard birds allow enthusiasts to feed and observe as time permits. This book is for the curious who would like a simple way—one that doesn't take much time—to learn about the birds in their neighborhoods.

Some people wonder about the birds that move through their backyards but have never had the time to learn about them. Home office workers wonder what those four birds are that perch on the holly tree. Children need projects for a spring break. Some people draw strength from the constant, comforting presence of birds. If you are one of these people, this book is for you.

For many, connecting to the natural world around us begins with birds. Birds, adapted to many different habitats, are the most obvious representatives of this natural world. Birds are the part of nature that takes up residence on the ledges of our apartment buildings and in the shrubs of suburban homes.

Overview

This book introduces birds frequently seen in North American backyards. Chapter 1 provides an overview of groups of birds. The birds are assembled, not into "hereditary" families based on DNA, but into "activities groups." Think of groups as being birds with similar interests, rather than related species.

For those who wish to bring more birds to the backyard, or lure the birds to better viewing spots, an introduction to attracting backyard birds and a simple bird feeding setup is the subject of Chapter 2. Water, food, and the other reasons that birds visit your yard are revealed. A basic feeder and watering setup and basic maintenance tips are covered in this chapter. Think "quick start" guide, rather than instructional manual.

Chapter 3 is a roster of the 50 most frequently seen birds at North American feeders. Their names, appearance and identifying marks, their diets, behavior notes, and the types of nests they build are included. In addition, you can find which of the five regions you live in and key on the most frequently seen birds in your area.

In the bird world, feather care, migration, breeding, and feeding are the

Evening grosbeaks can be seen across most of the US and Canada, depending on the season.

key activities. Knowing a bit about each of these life-and-death issues increases your appreciation of things you never imagined you'd see outside your window. Chapter 4 gets you started on learning bird behavior basics.

When you know habitat, you can create it. Food, water, shelter, and a place to rear young make a habitat that will fill with birds. The more combinations you have, the more diverse the birds and other natural wonders that will reside near your home. Chapter 5 introduces your family to a broad array of activities, including experimenting with feeders and waterers, keeping different types of lists, connecting with people of similar interests, and doing seasonal kids' activities about backyard birds.

Challenges arise in every pastime. Backyard bird activities are no different. You'll encounter problems with a pet or wildlife. You'll be hooked on landscaping for the birds. You'll become obsessed with attracting a particular type of bird that doesn't visit your feeder. Birds will show behaviors you don't understand. A baby bird with call at you pitifully from across the lawn. Chapter 6 helps you solve these common problems.

At the end is a list of resources: places to obtain feed and equipment; organizations of interest to backyard bird enthusiasts; books on natural history, identification, and bird behavior; and online sites you can visit.

Bird Groups

Sorting through the groups of birds may seem difficult at first. As you begin to recognize the birds that come to your yard repeatedly, seeing similarities within the groups is easier. Being able to identify a bird is the first step to enjoying it more. You'll see it

Use Your Eyes First

Watch birds the way a movie director shows a movie scene, the "long shot" first. You see birds in the trees, the feeders, on the backyard fence, your birdbath.

A flock of birds lands. Are there three or 33? What did the birds do first? Did they feed on the ground or on the tube feeder? Did they call as they came to the feeder? Did the birds already at the feeder stay or go?

Then go for the details. Is the bird bigger or smaller than a robin? Bright colors or dull? Any markings? Can you see the type of beak?

Use your eyes rather than binoculars. By starting with the "long view," you learn what the bird is doing and the direction in which it is moving, and you get a general impression of the bird. Then bring your binoculars up to see more details of the bird's markings and exactly what the bird is eating.

more vividly, recognize it when you see it again; you'll start to see patterns in its behavior over time, and you'll be able to read about it and understand more about it.

Questions that make identification easier include:

- How large is the bird?
- What was the bird doing when you saw it?
- What did you notice most about the bird?

The answers to these questions allow you to move the bird you want to identify into nontraditional but easy-to-understand groupings: birds that cling to trees, which are mostly woodpeckers; small colorful birds, which are mostly finches; medium to large black birds and jays; the hawks; and birds seen mostly on the ground.

If you see a bird clinging to a tree trunk, it is most likely a woodpecker, like this red-bellied woodpecker.

Birds That Cling to Trees: Mostly Woodpeckers

The most frequently seen birds that cling to trees are woodpeckers. These birds have two toes that point forward, two toes that point backward. Their bills are straight and are adapted for drilling holes and grabbing insects from small places under or between pieces of bark.

Woodpeckers will come to suet feeders during the winter when sap has stopped and insects aren't available. These birds use their tail feathers to support them as they move around a tree. The downy woodpecker is the most common example throughout North America.

Nuthatches, which act similarly by clinging to trees, are acrobatic birds with gray-blue backs and very short tails. They share the woodpeckers' habit of grabbing insects with thin, pointed beaks. Typically feeding upside down on the tree, the nuthatch will hold its position when another bird makes an alarm call. When it does, it looks just like a bump on a log.

To open seeds, nuthatches wedge them into a crevice and hammer with their beaks. Frequent backyard feeder visitors, nuthatches are fascinating to watch. They are also among the birds that, with patience, you can train to eat from your hand.

Small Colorful Birds: Mostly Finches

Because we're calling this category "small, colorful birds," the less colorful finches are not included. We add into this group chickadees, an entertaining family of birds that are colorful in a subtle and beautiful way.

The largest finches are grosbeaks, named for their large, cone-shaped beak. Evening grosbeaks—yellow, olive, and black—live in the north and west. Pine grosbeaks—a rosy red—live in spruce and fir forests. Grosbeaks are slow moving but acrobatic birds with little fear of humans.

Medium to Large Black Birds and Jays

Jays, like their relatives the crows and ravens, are intelligent and loud. Other birds scatter when these bullies arrive at the feeder. In the east, the blue jay is a crested bird with barred wings and tail and a white belly. West of the Rocky Mountains, the Steller's jay is darker, from a bright blue to

black, and lacking the white accents. The crestless western scrub-jay is often called the "camp robber."

Jays harass crows, hawks, owls, and your pets. Jays sound the alarm when cats or snakes arrive. In the spring, they dive through the trees and rob birds of eggs and nestlings.

Jays, crows, and ravens all cache foods, including nuts and acorns. If you have young trees spouting in your garden, odds are most of them were forgotten caches from your jay, crow, or raven friends.

Hawks

The hawks seen in backyards are those that hunt birds for a living. Their keen eyesight catches motion from far above. The

The Expert Knows

Beaks

Birds' beaks come in different sizes and shapes because they are food extractors whose features are based on the birds' diet. Some beaks, like that of the northern cardinal (top), are like nutcrackers, forcible enough to open large seeds. Birds like the American robin (center) have slim beaks, like chopsticks that serve as probes or tongs. Woodpeckers (bottom) have bills that break rotting wood and drill into trees to find insects. Their bills are like ice picks.

most common hawks in urban and suburban backyards are sharp-shinned hawks. These agile fliers hunt mice, rats, and squirrels in addition to birds.

Hawks have strong beaks, designed to tear flesh, and sharp talons. When hawks strike, they squeeze with their talons. Their beaks are shaped to allow them to pluck the feathers off a dead bird, or tear into the flesh of a squirrel. This natural process in the food chain may be easier to accept if you realize that these birds usually kill their prey instantly and that the prey they take is usually slow or weak. This is nature's way of assuring that the fittest birds breed each year.

Birds Seen Mostly on the Ground

Ground feeders include birds that naturally eat on the ground, such as robins. Other birds frequently seen on the ground include mourning doves.

This group also includes sparrows, a group of birds you may want to sort out later, after you fall in love with them. All sparrows have small, cone-shaped beaks, as is typical of seed eaters, but the sparrows can be confusing to identify. These birds eat weed seeds and work hard to keep your garden clean. Sparrows use a back-and-forth motion to scratch at seeds and

are quick to take flight. These birds are also enthusiastic bathers.

Our Example Bird: The American Robin

In learning anything new, you have to start somewhere. Let's start with one bird that is easy to distinguish: the American robin.

Most people, looking at a robin, would describe this as a bird that hangs out on the lawn, hops, and pecks at the grass. We put the bird into the category of "birds seen mostly on the ground." When you look at a picture of a robin, you don't know this. You see a picture of a bird with a dark head, an orange front, and a white ring around the eye. Maybe you notice the yellow beak; maybe not.

Fox sparrows and other sparrows are often seen on the ground.

Once you put the bird into the category of "birds seen mostly on the ground," you can page through Chapter 3 and see whether you can identify the bird. However, identifying the bird is only the beginning. Noticing what the bird does may be the real reason to keep looking.

Robins have quite a few interesting behaviors and traits. Roland Wauer, in his book *The American Robin,* says that robins have an average body temperature of 109.7°F (43.2°C); by comparison, normal human temperature is only 98.6°F (37°C). They have about 2,900 feathers, and can fly from 17 to 32 miles per hour (27 to 51.5 kph). Wauer renders the robin's song as: "cheer-up, cheerily, cheer-up, cheer-up, cheerily." Robins are dedicated parents, feeding an average brood a total of 3.2 pounds (1.5 kg) of food in 356 feedings per day, every day during the 13 to 15 days it takes until their babies are able to leave the nest.

Roland Wauer has watched robins for a long time. You probably wouldn't count the feathers, but over a season you might learn that robins lay blue eggs; that they fly straight ahead, rather than bouncing up and down as they fly, zig-zagging, or hovering like hummingbirds; and that they cock their heads sideways when hunting to see an insect, spider, or earthworm better. In the fall, you might see robins eat berries that have fermented, making them intoxicated. They flap and stagger, but recover enough to fly safely by the next day.

FAMILY-FRIENDLY TIP

Beak Art

Here's an artistic and fun activity for kids that will teach them about bird beaks.

1. Find the pictures of the American robin, the northern cardinal, and the downy woodpecker. Draw the shape of the robin's bill. Try the cardinal's bill next. Finally, draw the woodpecker's bill.
2. Use paint or crayons to color in the bill, also called a beak.
3. Cut around the beak to make your own silhouette.
4. Which one do you like best, and why?
5. Now, take a walk in your backyard or spend an afternoon watching the feeder. Do you see a bird with a bill shaped like one you drew?

A combination of watching and, when you're in the mood, reading about birds is the best education. Be sure to notice the size of the robin when you see one next. Throughout this book, we'll discuss birds as larger or smaller than a robin.

As you spend more time looking at your backyard birds, you'll notice their habits, their daily pattern of activities, and what is normal behavior for a certain type of bird. Happily, the more time you spend looking at birds, the more you'll notice and the more birds you'll recognize. You'll notice the groups first and then learn to distinguish the bird species in that group. Later, you'll distinguish male birds from females.

The Kinds of Backyards Birds Live In

Birds tend to remain where they have food, water, and cover that meet their needs. If you live on a farm surrounded by prairie grass, the birds you'll see will be different from the birds your friend sees from her New York City window ledge or your cousin reports from his backyard in the Virginia mountains.

In addition to a backyard being located either east or west of the Rocky Mountains, the habitats or kinds of backyards, can be further defined by elevation, amount of water, and the types of plants that grow in them.

Another description of your backyard habitat is called the ecosystem or biome. Ecosystem refers to the collective natural and geographical features in an area. For example, in the Rocky Mountains, evergreen trees flourish, and the birds that eat the seeds of pine cones do well

here. This ecosystem, called the coniferous forest, is very different from the desert southwest, which has few trees and very little water. You may live in the coniferous forest, deciduous forest, grassland, oak woodland, pinyon-juniper woodland, chaparral, sagebrush, or scrub desert.

These ecosystems determine which birds could be physically present in your area. Which birds are present in your specific backyard or window ledge depend on the habitat that nature or your landscaping provides. If there's nothing to eat, no cover, and nowhere to bathe, your backyard will be empty. If that's the case, no worries; this book will help you fix that.

A habitat can be described as the plant community within an ecosystem in which you find a bird. Within the deciduous forest of the eastern United States, you find freshwater marshes surrounded by cattails, clusters of oak forest, and miles of treeless lawn. Red-winged blackbirds more often live among cattails than in the oak forest, and American robins more often feed on the suburban lawn than in cattails.

The American robin is familiar to most people, so it will serve as the example bird in this book.

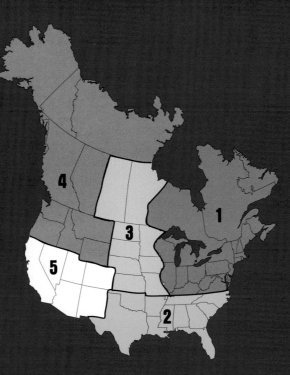

Bird Regions

The Rocky Mountains are the big divide for birds in North America. In addition to this land barrier, types of plant communities common to each area create regions. Different birds frequent these five regions of North America:

Region 1: Atlantic-Great Lakes
Includes Labrador, Newfoundland, Nova Scotia, Ontario, Prince Edward Island, Quebec, Connecticut, Delaware, District of Columbia, Illinois, Indiana, Kentucky, Maine, Maryland, Massachusetts, Michigan, New Hampshire, New Jersey, New York, Ohio, Pennsylvania, Rhode Island, Vermont, Virginia, West Virginia, Wisconsin

Region 2: Southeast and South Central
Includes Alabama, Arkansas, Florida, Georgia, Louisiana, Mississippi, North Carolina, Oklahoma, South Carolina, Tennessee, Texas

Region 3: Mid and North Central
Includes Manitoba, Saskatchewan, Iowa, Kansas, Minnesota, Missouri, Nebraska, North Dakota, South Dakota

Region 4: Northern Pacific and Rockies
Includes Alberta, British Columbia, Idaho, Montana, Oregon, Washington, Wyoming

Region 5: California and the Southwest
Includes Arizona, California, Colorado, New Mexico, Nevada, Utah

Chapter 2

Attracting

Backyard Birds

People attract birds so they can look at them; their colors, their habits, and the sense of life they give compel us to watch them. Morning birdsong before we rise starts the day on a positive note. Winter mornings become more pleasurable if we can watch colorful birds feed as we have our breakfast. Our common birds hold uncommon beauty and endless fascination for us.

What attracts birds to the backyard? Look at your backyard. Do you have birds that visit regularly? Perhaps you want birds in your backyard, but nothing you do seems to attract them.

This chapter examines the basics for those who wish to bring more birds to the backyard or lure the birds to better viewing spots. It provides basic information about water, food, and other factors that attract birds to visit your yard. This quick-start summary gives a basic feeder and water setup. Basic maintenance tips are included. More extensive information is included in Chapters 5.

The four elements that attract birds are food, cover, water, and a place to rear young. You may already have this habitat through existing plantings and natural features outside your home. Alternatively, you could create areas on a patio, on a window ledge, or in your yard to provide these bird-attracting features.

Water

Birds, like athletes, need a lot of energy. They also need plenty of water each day to help them use their food to provide this needed energy. In addition, water is important to bird feather care.

Especially in dry areas, or when water sources are frozen, standing or running water is more attractive to birds than food.

The Basics

The source of water does not need to be fancy. A terra cotta flowerpot saucer is adequate. The most practical birdbath is the one you may remember from your grandmother's yard: a concrete bowl set on a pedestal. This type of birdbath is sturdy and long lasting.

Whatever the container, the important point is that the bowl is shallow and rough bottomed so that birds can keep their footing. One inch (2.5 cm) of water is all that's required. In fact, deeper water is not attractive from the bird's perspective.

Water features will attract just as many birds as feeders will.

Best-Bet Birdbaths

The birdbath we all remember is the one in our grandmother's yard, the one on the pedestal made of concrete. The great aspect of this bath is that the bowl is shallow and the texture of the bowl is rough, giving birds a good foothold. Placed near cover, these baths offer birds a superior platform for bathing. Common backyard birds attracted to this type of bath include chickadees, house finches, goldfinches, grackles, robins, and house sparrows.

Placing a birdbath on the ground will also attract birds, especially if elevated cover is nearby in case the birds need it to escape predators. Woodland birds are more comfortable with these baths. Platforms that sway in the breeze are less satisfactory than anchored baths because the swinging baths lose their water.

The major mistake most people make with birdbaths is overfilling. Birds need 1 inch (2.5 cm) of water to bathe in, and no more. Change the water frequently. Baths need regular cleaning to eliminate algae and mosquito larvae that grow in standing water. Scouring pads can eliminate the algae. Some bird lovers store their scouring tool on a wire looped around the bath for quick cleanups.

The sound of water attracts birds more than does standing water. A simple way to provide moving water is to suspend a plastic milk jug with a small hole in it to drip water into a

How to Maintain a Birdbath

1. Pour out the old water.
2. Remove debris and detritus.
3. Scrub with soap and water.
4. Disinfect if needed. Rinse.
5. Refill to water level of 1 inch (2.5cm).

Easy tip: Use a nozzle on the garden hose set to a brisk stream to remove algae, leaves, and bird droppings in between scrubbings.

saucer. Professional wildlife photographers often get great pictures of wild birds attracted to close range using this method.

Commercial misters or backyard watering systems send sprays of water into the air. Birds may be drawn to fly through the spray, or they can bathe on the leaves of plants misted by watering systems.

Wintertime bathing is more problematic if you live in an area that has subfreezing temperatures. Use heaters if necessary in special birdbaths made for this use. Never, ever put antifreeze or anything else into the birdbath to keep the water from freezing. While these substances keep metal parts working in the cold, living creatures die from drinking them. The result will be death of your treasured backyard birds and any other creature that either drinks from or bathes in your birdbath and licks or preens fur or feathers.

An evening grosbeak and a cardinal feeding at a tube feeder.

Feeders and Feeding

Birds need a large amount of food relative to their size because they have a high metabolic rate. Hummingbirds, for example, eat one-and-a-half to three times their weight each day. Young birds eat constantly because they have a very short time in which to grow to maturity. A bird hatched in May must be ready to migrate in September.

Birds also replace their feathers annually, meaning they must grow a completely new set of feathers at least once each year. This requires more energy than growing hair or fur does for mammals. Finally, flight demands a lot of fuel.

Starter Feeder

Start with one hanging tube feeder such as the "Droll Yankee." Tube feeders are heavy-duty plastic or glass cylinders, with a closed top and a bottom fitted with perches and feeding openings. The top is removable to allow you to fill the feeder with seed. Perches allow the birds to reach through feeding openings and pull out the seeds.

The "Droll Yankee" has an especially good design and sturdy construction.

The most important aspect of feeder design is to keep the seed dry and to provide a place for the bird to perch. Other features such as color or material are less important to the bird. The feeder must be positioned near cover that provides a safe hiding place. Otherwise, birds will not come.

If you want to add another "feeder" to your starter set, place seed on the ground, on a table, or in a ground feeder. A suet feeder, a simple wire cage on a nearby tree trunk, if you have a tree-filled backyard, is a nice third option.

Selecting Your Feeder

Despite the bewildering array of options, your selection of a bird feeder need not be complicated. The hundreds of feeders available all fall into a few basic categories. If your feeders are well constructed, they'll be easy to fill and clean.

Feeders should protect the seed from rain, wind, and snow. In addition, good feeders allow any water that gets inside to drain away from the seed. A simply constructed, quality feeder made of wood, metal, or plastic will last you for years.

What To Feed

In snowy winter areas, those birds that rely on insects have migrated to warmer places. Seed- and berry-eating birds remain in North American yards. Because of this, seed is the primary feeding ingredient.

Experienced feeders suggest that you purchase only the seed that attracts the birds you want. If you feed seed mixes, birds will sweep the less desirable seeds

Black-oil sunflower seed is one of the best general-purpose seeds.

(milo, flax, rapeseed, cracked corn, or canary seed) aside. This seed, on the ground below the feeders, will attract rats and mice. Rather than purchase cheap seed mixes that create problems, purchase a higher-quality black-oil sunflower seed–based feed to attract the first group of birds you'll love.

Black-oil sunflower seed in a tube feeder attracts chickadees, finches, and nuthatches. If you decide to place a second feeder, use Nyjer (pronounced nye-jyr) seed in a tube feeder to attract goldfinches.

Placing Your First Feeder

Consider the following factors when placing your first feeder:
- **You want to see the birds.** Place your feeder in front of a window where you and your family spend time.
- **Birds need cover,** such as bushes or trees, as a place to retreat from danger. Be sure cover is available no closer than 3 and no further than 10 feet (1 to 3 m) from your feeder.
- **Birds need protection from the wind and rain.** From which direction does wind and rain come? Place your feeder to shelter your birds from these elements.

Recipe for Disinfectant

To make a cup of disinfecting solution, put on rubber gloves and mix 2 tablespoons of chlorine bleach with 1 cup (236 mL) of water. Stir. Caution: Do not allow the bleach solution to touch your skin. If it does, rinse with cool water for several minutes.

Seed-Storing Basics

When you store seed properly, you make the most of your bird-feeding dollars and create the opportunity for more fun. Why is the location of seed storage important?

Convenience is one reason. If you have an upper-level kitchen window feeder, store the seed beneath the sink in a metal container. If you have a large backyard, store feed close to your back door. Seed storage places should be easy to clean and out of the reach of hungry animals like squirrels. The storage area should be a dry place that is as cool as possible, such as an unheated garage.

To prevent rodents and insects from dining on the birds' seed, use metal cans with tight-fitting lids. For your convenience, try labeling the cans with a waterproof marker.

Cleaning Feeders

Every time you refill your feeder, remove any seed that is stuck or damp before refilling. Wet seed rapidly turns moldy, and moldy seed does not attract birds. Worse, layering new seed on top of moldy seed yields more moldy seed.

To prevent bird disease and to keep your feeder area neat, a thorough, routine cleaning every 3 months is best. To clean feeders thoroughly:

1. Remove the wet or spoiled seed as you always do in refilling,
2. Scrape off bird droppings.
3. Scrub your feeder with soap and water, especially around perches and feeding shelves.
4. After cleaning, rinse, and then disinfect. Wear rubber gloves when you apply a solution of 1 part chlorine bleach to 9 parts water.
5. Let stand for 15 minutes.
6. Rinse thoroughly, and allow the feeder to dry.

Once your feeder is clean, be sure to rake or sweep the area under your feeder or use a water spray to clean your deck or patio. Dispose of sunflower seed hulls in your trash. Sunflower seed hulls contain a natural chemical that may keep other seeds from germinating.

Supplies can make the job easier. Some feeder watchers use a spatula to remove wet seed. A scrub brush for removing caked-on droppings helps on the outside of the feeder. Using a long-handled brush to clean the inside of your tube feeder can help you reach into tight spaces. Use a different brush for applying the bleach solution. Choose inexpensive brushes, but ensure that they fit into the remote corners of your feeders.

Other Inducements

Few things are more fun than watching a pair of backyard birds raise a family. From the nest-building stage through the babies growing up and flying off, something exciting is always happening. You'll increase the probability of seeing nesting and breeding behavior if you provide inducements. Besides the basics of food and water, birds are attracted by some other comforts you can provide.

Nesting Material

The variety of nesting materials birds use is astonishing. Some birds favor white feathers, such as the soft downy feathers from chickens, ducks, or geese. Others love pieces of string or yarn. If you decide to provide string or yarn, cut the pieces 6 inches (15 cm) long or less, to keep them from wrapping around bird legs or wings.

FAMILY-FRIENDLY TIP

Do-It-Yourself Feeder Projects

Feeders can be as simple or as complicated as you and your children's construction skills can handle. Here are a few simple ideas that any child older than a toddler can work on. Your local library or some online sources included in the Resources section may provide more complex plans for building feeders with your family.

Suet
The simplest suet feeder is a mesh bag, like those that hold onions or garlic from the supermarket. Place the suet inside the bag. Using a length of wire, either secure the bag to a tree trunk or suspend the bag from a branch. A child can help fill the bag and select a spot for you to hang the feeder.

Nectar (Sugar and Water)
If you do not have a hummingbird feeder, suspend a shallow red plate from a length of wire. Pour nectar into the plate, leaving the edge dry as a perch for the birds. Depending on your child's age, he can mix the nectar or hang the feeder.

Seed
Cover a pinecone with peanut butter. Roll the covered cone in seed. Suspend from a wire. This one is fun for any child.

How to Maintain a Feeder

1. Remove the old seed, suet, or sugar water solution.
2. Remove the bird poop or other detritus from the outside of the feeder by scraping.
3. Scrub with soap and water to remove the organic material.
4. Disinfect the feeder with bleach solution.
5. Check and repair any loose pieces.
6. Refill with seed.

Easy tip: Store cleaning materials near the seed, including a metal spatula for scraping, a scrub brush, and the disinfectant.

Tiny twigs, 4 to 6 inches (10 to 15 cm) long, form the basis for many nests. Birds use brush piles or shrubs as a source for these important materials.

Mane or tail hair from horses, or dog or cat combings are fibers used by nest-making birds. Dried moss is a different but equally interesting material. Place your nest materials inside a hanging basket. The basket or holder can be hung anywhere your birds regularly visit in your yard, such as a favorite feeder or a well-used bush or deck railing.

Cover

Cover usually consists of plants surrounding the home that allow a bird to perch in thick brush, where predators would find it difficult to enter, or at a height that is out of predators' reach. For this reason, clearing all the brush in your yard deprives birds of valuable cover. You might use your Christmas tree or pruned branches to create a brush pile that will protect many different types of birds, including ground-nesting birds.

Cover nearby will increase the number and variety of birds visiting your feeders and bird baths. If you live in the range where quail roam, these ground-living birds will be attracted to these brush piles.

Houses and Roosting Places

Birds' nests are cradles for rearing young birds. Birds' nests are not homes. Birds take shelter in an activity called roosting. At night, birds find a safe place and stay there in the protection of cover. On cold nights, some birds, such as chickadees, huddle together in tree cavities for warmth. Other birds, such as crows, roost in large groups at night, for protection and companionship. Birds also roost in dense cover or cavities during days of bad or cold weather.

Whether or not birds decide to nest in your yard, they will appreciate having places to roost. No matter what kinds of outbuildings or covered eaves or ledges your home has, these may be used by birds as shelters, if not for nesting, then for evening roosting.

You can create bottomless birdhouses or other structures in your yard to provide roosting places for birds. Dead trees make excellent roosts and nesting places. If you have a dead tree in your yard, consider leaving a majority of the trunk, taking down only the portion of the tree that presents a danger to those using the yard. Cavity-nesting birds will use the dead tree, also called a snag.

Chapter 5 contains the critical information needed for creating bird-specific birdhouses.

Bird houses give birds places to nest in your yard. Here, a house wren feeds a fledgling.

Sample Observation Chart

July 4, 2007

Hour	Number of Feeder Visitors
5:00 a.m.	3
6:00 a.m.	20
7:00 a.m.	22
8:00 a.m.	10
9:00 a.m.	4
10:00 a.m.	2
11:00 a.m.	5
12:00 a.m.	4
1:00 p.m.	0
2:00 p.m.	3
3:00 p.m.	4
4:00 p.m.	1
5:00 p.m.	10
6:00 p.m.	27
7:00 p.m.	19
8:00 p.m.	1

Best Times to Observe Feeding

Typically, birds are most active just before and at dawn. The hours of activity change as the seasons do. Use sunrise as your guide. A fun project can be learn which hours are most productive in your own backyard. The hours will change from month to month.

Birds like to eat in the hour before dusk to fuel their bodies for the night's roost. Use sunset as a guide, and watch for birds in the hour before the sun sets. Record how many birds you see during this time. If you're home during the day, record once each hour and compare. Your chart will look something like the one shown here.

Chapter 3

The Top Fifty

Backyard Birds

In this chapter, we put North America's top 50 feeder birds into the groups of birds we considered in Chapter 1. The 50 types of birds are called species. Species of birds are similar to breeds of dogs. Each bird species is made up of individuals that are similar in appearance, habits, voice, and DNA. The difference between birds and dogs is that birds tend to breed with their own kind rather than being less discriminating, as dogs are.

As you spend more time looking at your backyard birds, you'll notice their habits, what they do at various times of the day, and what activities are normal for that type of bird.

For example, chickadees fly in, take a seed, and fly off to eat it. Goldfinches spend time at the feeder with the thistle seed. Sparrows scratch around on the ground for millet.

Another point to be aware of is that birds molt, or replace their feathers, once or twice each year. Most birds have brighter colors in summer and duller colors in winter, to blend in and escape predators. Some birds molt into a breeding plumage that looks very different from their nonbreeding coloration. The yellow-rumped warbler is a good example of this color change.

North America is within the normal range of more than 600 bird species, making the task of learning about all bird species seem impossible for a beginner. Using the Project FeederWatch list of the top 50 feeder birds on the North American continent, we've pared the list to a reasonable starting number of birds that people see at their feeders or in their backyards near feeders in the United States and

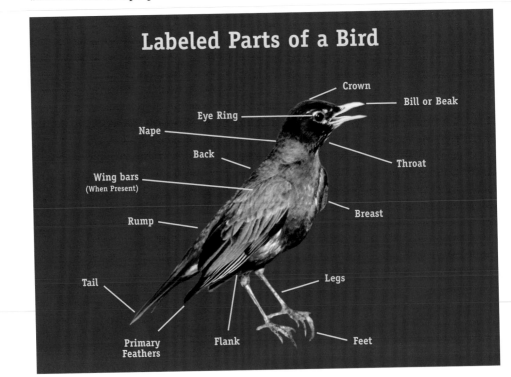

Labeled Parts of a Bird

Crown

Bill or Beak

Eye Ring

Nape

Back

Throat

Wing bars
(When Present)

Breast

Rump

Tail

Legs

Primary
Feathers

Flank

Feet

Canada. (Later in the book, we discuss some additional birds in each region that did not make the Top 50 list, but are common for that region.)

The other birds in North America are no less worthy for inclusion; it's just that you have to start somewhere. Getting familiar with birds is like moving to a new neighborhood. At first, only your next-door neighbors look familiar. Then you begin to know which members of the neighborhood are couples. Then you pair the couples with their homes.

Learning about birds is similar. You see which ones hang out in the evergreen trees, which ones hop on the ground, and which ones never leave tree trunks except to come to a suet feeder.

To help with some of the profiles, a photograph of our American Robin shows labels of the most common parts of the body.

The Top 50 Feeder Bird Profiles

The profiles and photographs together give you a starting point of knowledge about these 50 backyard birds most frequently seen by the volunteers from Project FeederWatch. The profiles are not all inclusive, but each one provides important information for identification and feeding, as well as additional information for entertainment and education.

Male versus Female

Some male birds have brighter colors than do females, especially in the spring. Females need a camouflaged appearance so that they can sit still and nearly invisible while incubating eggs, even with predators nearby.

Males use their bright colors to attract mates. Less colorful females judge the male's fitness to breed based on his feather quality.

Males don't develop their bright colors until their second spring. Therefore, male birds younger than 1 year old look more like their mothers than their fathers.

Example Profile

Name: Each profile uses the American Ornithologist's Union or AOU common name for the bird. The American Ornithologists' Union, a group of dedicated professional and amateur ornithologists (people who study birds), gives each North American bird species its official name. Sometimes this group changes a name because of new things learned about the bird. This group also assigns the scientific nomenclature (the Latin name) for each bird species. These Latin names follow the common name.

More About Beaks

Beaks, also called bills, indicate the type of food a bird typically eats. The birds mentioned in this book have beaks that fall into three general categories: triangle, chopstick, or hook-shaped. Birds with triangle-shaped beaks tend to eat seeds. Birds with chopstick-shaped beaks generally eat a variety of foods, including insects or worms. Hook-shaped beaks belong to hawks.

Size: Described in relation to the American Robin. The size, in inches and centimeters, is measured from tip of bill to tip of tail.

Habitat: Refers to the type of plant community preferred as living area by the species.

Foods: Includes both usual foods gathered in the wild and the preferred food at feeders.

Behaviors: Gives a clue to activities you might see the bird do while you're watching.

Marks: A word-based description of the bird, accompanying the photograph and pointing out particular marks of distinction.

Nests: Describes the type of nest and something about the nest construction.

Voice: Included when the voice or call is distinctive, to help a beginning birder locate particular birds.

Confused with: This entry is intended to help you distinguish among birds of similar species.

Range: Gives the distribution of the bird across North America. Because a bird is present in a range does not mean that it is seen uniformly throughout that range. Some birds can be found only in appropriate habitats within their range.

Some profiles include "factoids," interesting tidbits about a bird that may increase your pleasure in seeing that bird in your yard.

Birds That Cling to Trees: Mostly Woodpeckers

Downy Woodpecker
(Picoides pubescens)

Size: Smaller than a robin, 6 inches (15 cm)
Habitat: Woods, farmlands, suburbs.
Foods: Insects under tree bark; suet and sunflower seed at feeders.

Behaviors: Hops up and around tree trunks looking for insects. In spring, taps or drums on surfaces as a part of courtship.
Marks: White-spotted black wings and black head stripes. Remainder of body white overall. Heavy, pointed bill. Male has red spot on back of head.

Nests: Excavates holes in standing dead trees.

Confused with: Hairy woodpecker. The downy is smaller, with white spots on its outer tail feathers and a bill half the length of its head.

Range: All regions.

Hairy Woodpecker
(Picoides villosus)

Size: Smaller than a robin, 9 inches (24 cm)

Habitat: Woods, farmlands, suburbs. Prefers evergreen trees.

Foods: Insects under tree bark, sap; suet, sunflower seed, and occasionally nectar and fruit at feeders.

Behaviors: Pairs form in winter. Male and female drum duets; courtship appears to be a chase followed by friendly gestures, including a hovering flight and perching next to one another. Excavates nests over 20 days.

Marks: Gray-white breast, belly, back, mustache, and eyebrow. Black wings with white spots. Male has red spot at back of head.

Nests: Excavates nest in living trees.

Confused with: Downy woodpecker. Hairy is larger, with a bill as long as its head.

Range: All regions.

Red-Bellied Woodpecker
(Melanerpes carolinus)

Size: Slightly smaller than robin at 9 inches (24 cm)

Habitat: Woodlands, parks, suburbs.

Foods: Insects under tree bark and acorns, fruit in summer; suet and sunflower seed at feeders.

Behaviors: Usually works upward on tree trunks. Occasionally feeds on ground. Raises crest during courtship.

Marks: Zebra-striped on back, red nape, white rump patch. In males, red extends to top of head. Buff-colored breast, belly, flanks.

Nests: Excavates holes in living trees in 10 days; sometimes uses existing hole or birdhouse. Starlings compete for the cavity.

Confused with: Barred back and lack of complete red head distinguishes it from the red-headed woodpecker; red head marking distinguishes it from sapsuckers.

Range: East of Rockies in Regions 1-3.

Pileated Woodpecker
(Dryocopus pileatus)

Size: Larger than robin, 16 inches (41 cm)

Habitat: Mature forest, suburbs with mature large trees.

Foods: Carpenter ants, other insects, fruit; suet at feeders.

Behaviors: Voice sounds like hands clapping. Hand clap sometimes causes bird to call.

Marks: Black with red crest; white moustache, neck line, under wings; male has red mustache mark. Whole crest is red in males. Female has only half the crest red.

Nests: Excavates in standing dead wood over 15 feet high.

Confused with: Unmistakable. Much larger than other woodpeckers; red crest and white markings distinguish it from the crow.

Range: All regions.

Red-Breasted Nuthatch
(Sitta canadensis)

Size: Smaller than robin, 4 inches (11.5 cm)

Habitat: Prefers evergreen woods with decaying trees.

Foods: Insects. In winter may take conifer seeds; at feeders, sunflower seed and suet.

Behaviors: Moves headfirst down the tree trunk, looking for insects under the bark or in the cracks between the pieces of bark. Pairs remain together through winter if adequate food is present.

Marks: Dark crown, white face, black eye stripe, rust-colored breast. Short, stubby tail. Short, very pointed bill.

Nests: Roots, grass, moss in excavated hole.

Confused with: Brown creepers spiral up trees from base to branches and have a streaky back. Chickadees have longer tails.

Range: All regions.

White-Breasted Nuthatch
(Sitta carolinensis)

Size: Smaller than robin, 6 inches (15 cm)

Habitat: Woods, especially deciduous, such as oak. Prefers mature forest.

Foods: Insects and spiders, nuts in winter; at feeders, sunflower seed and suet.

Behaviors: Works down tree trunk head first, looking for insects under or between pieces of bark. Pairs maintain their feeding territory throughout the year.

Voice: Nasal whistle, *"whi whi..."*

Marks: Gray on back and wings, black cap, white face and underparts, rusty under tail. Short, stubby tail. Short, very pointed bill.

Nests: Twigs, bark, and fur placed in existing cavity.

Confused with: Red-breasted nuthatch is rusty below with white eye line.

Chickadees have longer tails. Brown creepers are streaked on back.
Range: All regions.

Small, Colorful Birds: Mostly Finches

American Goldfinch
(Carduelis tristis)

Size: Smaller than robin, 5 inches (13 cm)
Habitat: Open areas with some shrubs and trees, farms, gardens, suburbs.
Foods: Seeds, berries, insects; sunflower and thistle seed at feeders.
Behaviors: Usually seen in flocks. Bathes and drinks in birdbaths.
Marks: Yellow body, black wings, and tail. Male has black forehead.
Nests: Made of plant fibers, caterpillar webbing; up 4 feet (1.2 m) or higher in trees.
Confused with: Lesser goldfinch has all-yellow underparts and more white in wings.
Range: All regions.

Lesser Goldfinch
(Carduelis psaltria)
Size: Smaller than robin, 4 inches (11.5 cm)

Habitat: Wood edges, roadsides, gardens, parks.
Foods: Seeds, flower buds, berries; sunflower and thistle seed at feeders.
Behaviors: Frequent bathers, these birds chatter and squabble with one another but get along well with other species of their size. Intimidated by jays.
Marks: Males have black caps and wings with white patch. Yellow on breast and belly with green or black back. Females are olive green washed with yellow.
Nests: Bark strips, moss, plant stems in shrubs or trees.
Confused with: American Goldfinch has white under the tail, and the black on its head is on forehead only.
Range: 2 (Southeast and Central), 4 (Pacific Northwest and Rockies), 5 (California and Southwest).

Black-Capped/Carolina Chickadee
(Poecile atricapillus/P. carolinensis)

Note: The black-capped and Carolina chickadees, in the ranges of overlap, interbreed and are difficult to distinguish. Project FeederWatch treats these as a single species for data reporting.

Size: Smaller than robin, 5 inches (13 cm)

Habitat: Woods, farms, suburbs.

Foods: Insects, seeds, berries; suet and sunflower seed at feeders.

Behaviors: Hangs upside down; winters in small, often mixed flocks; uses birdbaths. Stores feeder seed in nearby trees.

Voice: Call sounds like *"chick-a-dee-dee-dee."* Songs are variations on "Three Blind Mice."

Marks: Black cap and throat. White cheek, gray back, clear breast, small bill.

Nests: Excavates cavity in standing rotted wood, uses holes or birdhouse.

Confused with: Chestnut-backed chickadee has sooty brown cap and chestnut back. Mountain chickadee has white eyebrow.

Range: All regions.

Chestnut-Backed Chickadee
(Poecile rufescens)

Size: Smaller than robin, 5 inches (13 cm)

Habitat: Evergreen or mixed woods.

Foods: Insects, seeds, berries; suet and sunflower seed at feeders.

Behaviors: Hangs upside down; winters in small, often mixed flocks;

uses birdbaths. Stores feeder seed in nearby trees.

Marks: Dark cap, eye stripe, and throat; red-brown back; gray breast and chestnut or gray flanks.

Nests: Moss, hair, feathers in natural cavity.

Confused with: Black-capped or Carolina chickadee has black cap and lacks chestnut. Mountain chickadee has white eyebrow.

Range: Regions 4 (Northern Pacific and Rockies) and 5 (California and the Southwest).

Mountain Chickadee
(Poecile gambeli)

Size: Smaller than robin, 5 1/2 inches (14 cm)

Habitat: Open evergreen forests in mountains.

Foods: Insects, seeds, berries; suet and sunflower seed at feeders.

Behaviors: Birdbath frequenter.

Marks: Black cap and throat; white cheek; white line over eye; gray breast, back, and flanks.

Nests: Wood chips, hair, feathers. Can excavate cavity in rotted wood of standing trees, uses holes or birdhouse.

Confused with: Black-capped or Carolina chickadee has black cap and lacks chestnut. Chestnut-backed chickadee has sooty brown cap and chestnut back. Both lack white line over eye.

Range: Regions 4 (Northern Pacific and Rockies) and 5 (California and the Southwest).

Tufted Titmouse
(Baeolophus bicolor)

Size: Smaller than robin, 6 inches (15 cm)

Habitat: Woods, suburbs.

Foods: Insects, berries, seeds; suet and sunflower seed at feeders.

Behaviors: Rarely squabbles with other birds. Takes sunflower seeds and nuts, holds them with its feet, and hammers with strong but small bill. In winter, titmice join with chickadees, kinglets, and yellow-rumped warblers in yards, searching for insects and larvae.

Voice: Titmice socialize with high-pitched voices. Courtship call includes a clear whistled call, that sounds like *"Peter, Peter, Peter."*

Marks: Gray bird with tufted crest. Flanks rusty.

Nests: Existing cavity or birdhouse.

Confused with: Resemble chickadees, with which they share small, plump size and acrobatic feeding, but chickadees have no crest.

Range: Regions 1 (Atlantic-Great Lakes), 2 (Southeast and South Central), 3 (Mid and North Central).

Northern Cardinal
(Cardinalis cardinalis)

Size: Smaller than robin, 8 1/2 inches (21.5 cm)

Habitat: Shrubs near open areas, open woods, suburban yards.

Foods: Insects, spiders, seeds, berries; sunflower seed at feeders.

Behaviors: Open feeders with large landing areas attract them. These birds come to the feeders before others in the morning, and visit feeder after other birds have left in the evening. They do not dine in crowds.

Marks: All red with pointed crest and black patch at base of red bill. Heavy conical bill. Females buff with some red on wings and tail.

Voice: Peterson describes *"what-cheer cheer cheer"* and *"whoit whoit whoit"* and *"birdy birdy birdy."*

33

Nests: Twigs and bark strips in dense shrubs.

Confused with: Males unmistakable. Females similar to pyrrhuloxia (Region 5). Gray back and yellow bill of pyrrhuloxia set this bird apart from female cardinals.

Range: Regions 1 (Atlantic-Great Lakes), 2 (Southeast and South Central), 3 (Mid and North Central). Cardinals are often reported in the southwest, although they are not on the most frequently seen bird list.

Common Redpoll
(Carduelis flammea)

Size: Smaller than robin, 5 inches (14 cm)

Habitat: Wood edges, mountain forests, aspen groves, suburbs.

Foods: Insects gathered in bushes and on the ground; at feeders black oil sunflower and Nyjer thistle.

Behaviors: Occur in flocks, clinging to weeds or flower stems to eat seeds.

Marks: Streaky brown body with rosy breast. A bright red cap on top of the head and black mask around bill distinguishes this bird.

Nests: Cavities made by other birds.

Confused with: House finch lacks black mask around bill.

Range: Regions 1 (Atlantic-Great Lakes), 3 (Mid and North Central), 4 (Northern Pacific and Rockies).

Factoid: Redpolls are finches that wander southward in winter. Some years they appear far south; other years only as far as southern Canada.

House Finch
(Carpodacus mexicanus)

female   male

Size: Smaller than robin, 6 inches (15 cm)

Habitat: Urban areas, suburbs, parks, canyons, brush.

Foods: Seeds, blossoms, fruits; sunflower and Nyjer seed at feeders.

Behaviors: Sips sap from broken maple and box elder twigs. Can also drink from hummingbird feeders. Bathes and drinks readily at birdbaths.

Marks: Male has red head and upper breast, brownish back, brown streaking on lower breast and sides. Female has uniform fine streaks on head, broad brown streaks on belly and breast.

Voice: Sings year round; a long and chatty warble.

Nests: Twigs and grass in trees, shrubs, hanging planters.

Confused with: Purple finch shows extensive purple. House finch color

restricted to head and upper breast, showing lots of streaking on breast and sides.
Range: All regions.

Purple Finch
(Carpodacus purpureus)

Size: Smaller than robin, 6 inches (15 cm)
Habitat: Mixed woods, evergreen forests, low mountain slopes, suburbs.
Foods: Seeds, buds, berries, insects; sunflower and Nyjer thistle seed at feeders.
Behaviors: In winter, travels in mixed flocks of 20 to 30 birds, including siskins and goldfinches.
Marks: Breast, back, and head red; little streaking on breast or sides. Female brown streaked and lacking red coloring. Broad white eyebrow, brown eye line, and white cheek. Male sometimes described as "a sparrow dipped in raspberry juice."
Nests: Twigs and grasses, 5 feet (1.5 m) and above in trees.
Confused with: House finch. Purplish color, rather than red or orange that extends over a majority of the body, not just concentrated on face and rump.
Range: All regions.

Yellow-Rumped Warbler
(Dendroica coronata)

Size: Smaller than robin, 5 inches (14 cm)
Habitat: Evergreen or mixed forests for breeding. Nearly anywhere in winter.
Foods: Insects, some berries; suet and fruit at feeders.
Behaviors: Moves continuously in treetops or among leaves looking for insects.
Voice: Slow warble.
Marks: Flash of white in tail and wings. These birds have a distinctive yellow rump, seen as the bird flits around the branches.
Nests: Grasses and twigs, placed over 5 feet (1.5 m) high in trees
Confused with: Distinctive in breeding plumage. In winter, its thin bill and yellow rump distinguish it from sparrows.
Range: All regions.

Ruby-Crowned Kinglet
(Regulus calendula)
Size: Smaller than robin, 4 inches (11.5 cm)
Habitat: Winter in woods and brushy edges, summer in evergreen forests.

Foods: Insects, sap, small berries; nectar at feeders.

Behaviors: Flits among tree branches in constant motion and seems unafraid of people. In winter, frequents mixed flocks of other birds such as chickadees, creepers, nuthatches, and titmice. Frequently flicks wings.

Voice: Beautiful loud melody.

Marks: Tiny, plump-appearing bird with small dark bill, a white circle around the eye, and no stripes on the head. The patch of red head feathers that gives the bird its name is rarely seen.

Nests: Moss, twigs; hung from branch.

Confused with: Hutton's vireo very similar, but has larger, thicker beak and lacks black below the lower wing bar.

Range: All regions.

Pine Grosbeak
(Pinicola enucleator)

Size: Smaller than robin, 9 inches (23 cm)

Habitat: Evergreen forests, mixed woods and fruiting trees.

Foods: Buds, fruit, seeds of conifers. Especially prefers crab apples, mountain-ash berries, pine seeds, and maple buds; sunflower seed at feeders

Behaviors: Tame and approachable in winter. Bathes in soft snow. Flocks of 5 to 25. Sometimes accompanies Bohemian waxwings.

Marks: Large winter finch with long tail. Males are dull rose-red and have dark wings with two white wing bars. Females are similar in overall markings except gray color with yellow rump.

Nests: Cuplike, bulky nests of moss, twigs, grass, and lichens.

Confused with: Purple finch is much smaller.

Range: 1 (Atlantic-Great Lakes), 3 (Mid and North Central), 4 (Pacific Northwest and Rockies), 5 (California and Southwest).

Evening Grosbeak
(Coccothraustes vespertinus)

Size: Smaller than robin, 8 inches (20 cm)

Habitat: Open areas with trees and shrubs in winter.

Foods: Insects, fruit, and seeds, maple sap, buds of

female

male

trees and shrubs; sunflower seed at feeders.

Behaviors: Sometimes seen on winter roads seeking salt. Very tame.

Marks: Plump and short tail, massive beak, yellow body, black and white wings, and bright yellow eyebrow. Females lack eyebrow and are duller overall.

Nests: Fragile cup of twigs and moss in tree.

Confused with: American goldfinch is much smaller.

Range: All regions.

Pine Siskin
(Carduelis pinus)

Size: Smaller than robin, 5 inches (13 cm)

Habitat: Evergreen or mixed woods, shrubs and thickets, suburbs.

Foods: Pine and alder seeds, weed seeds, insects, flower buds, nectar; sunflower and thistle seed at feeders.

Behaviors: Also fond of sap and sometimes uses nectar feeders.

Voice: Call is a buzzy *"zzhreeee."*

Marks: Male and female look alike: a streaky brown finch with yellow-barred wings that show noticeable yellow patches when they fly. Streaked back is a distinctive field mark distinguishing it from other finches.

Nests: Grasses and twigs in trees.

Confused with: American and lesser goldfinch females. Distinguished by small pointed beaks, thinner than a goldfinch's.

Range: All regions.

Factoids: Siskins are reported to predict storms by their frenetic eating beforehand. In some years, pine siskins never move south.

Medium to Large Black Birds and Jays

American Crow
(Corvus brachyrhynchos)

Size: Larger than robin, 18 inches (46 cm)

Habitat: From country to city in open woodlands where trees are available for roosting.

Foods: Omnivore. Scavenges refuse, road kill, crops, and fruit.

Behaviors: Crows gather in large groups and roost together at night. Very intelligent. Harass predators until they leave. Excellent detectors of hawks.

Marks: All-black bird with large black bill.

Voice: Noisy *"caw."*

Nests: Large collection of twigs high in tree or trunk fork.

Confused with: Common raven has a much larger bill and body. Ravens soar more, with wings straight out, and have a wedge-shaped tail.

Range: All regions.

Red-winged Blackbird
(Agelaius phoeniceus)

Size: Smaller than robin, 8 1/2 inches (21.5 cm)

Habitat: Marshes, moist meadows with tall grasses.

Foods: Insects, seeds; mixed seed at feeders.

Behaviors: Social, as reflected in their many different calls. Form mixed winter flocks with grackles, starlings, cowbirds.

Marks: Female brown above, heavily streaked brown below, sharp, pointed bill, whitish eyebrow. Male black with red epaulets and usually yellow streak at epaulet bottom edge.

Voice: A loud *"conk-a-ree."* Other calls include a *"check"* call to warn of danger, a *"tseert"* call that warns of aerial predators, and a *"tch tch tch"* call

given by males chasing females or arguing with other males.

Nests: Reeds and grasses attached to taller grasses or shrubs

Confused with: Any black bird without epaulets. Females similar to grackle, cowbird, other blackbird females.

Range: All regions.

Factoid: Possibly the most numerous land bird species in North America.

Common Grackle
(Quiscalus quiscula)

Size: Larger than robin, 12 inches (30.5 cm)

Habitat: Open areas with some trees such as parks or yards.

Foods: Seeds, insects, fruit, crustaceans, fish; mixed seed at feeders.

Behaviors: Whips aside leaf litter with its bill to find insects. Uses birdbaths.

Marks: Black with iridescent head, back, and belly. Yellow eye.

Nests: Grass and mud; in trees.

Confused with: Other grackles and blackbirds. Distinguished by light eye and small size from American crow; solid body color as compared to European starling; distinguished from blackbirds by length and heavy body

and bronze gloss on body.
Range: Regions 1 (Atlantic-Great Lakes), 2 (Southeast and South central), 3 (Mid and North Central)

European Starling
(Sturnus vulgaris)

Size: Smaller than a robin, 8 inches (20 cm)
Habitat: Cities and suburbs.
Foods: Japanese beetle, weevils, cutworms; feeders for suet and seed variety.

Behaviors: Travels in crowds, good imitator of sounds. Waddling gait. Pushes closed bill into the ground and opens to find prey.
Marks: Glossy black-purple body with pattern of white and gold stars in winter. Spots worn off by summer. Beak yellow in spring and summer, gray in fall.
Nests: Grass and feathers; in cavity such as tree hole, birdhouse, or ledge of building.
Confused with: Common grackle has a solid body color; distinguished from blackbirds by yellow bill.
Range: All regions.
Factoid: Today's large population of starlings in North America came from 60 starlings released in 1890 in New York City's Central Park by a man said to be obsessed with introducing all birds mentioned in the works of Shakespeare. Today the starling is well-established in every locale inhabited by man. Competitors with bluebirds, woodpeckers, and wrens for nest holes.

Common Raven
(Corvus corax)

Size: More than double the size of a robin, 24 inches (61 cm)
Habitat: Middle to high elevations, widespread outside cities and suburbs.

Foods: Omnivore. Scavenges carcasses but also kills rodents and insects. Follows predators to scavenge meals.
Behaviors: Travels in crowds, good imitator of sounds, caches food for later use. Aerial acrobat. Regurgitates pellets, the undigested bones and hair of rodents, as hawks do. Roosts communally in flocks of up to several hundred individuals.
Marks: Glossy black with long wings, wedge-shaped tail, and long, heavy bill. Throat and head feathers appear puffed.
Voice: Variety of low, harsh cronks and rattles.
Nests: Branches and twigs in sturdy large cup shape, sometimes on trees and on human-built structures. Old

nests used by hawks and owls.
Confused with: American crow. Raven 6 inches (15 cm) larger, with very large beak. In flight, crow has flat tail edge, and raven has wedge-shaped tail.
Range: All regions.
Factoid: Largest North American songbird, always at odds with crows.

Blue Jay
(Cyanocitta cristata)

Size: Larger than robin, 11 inches (28 cm)
Habitat: Woods and suburbs.
Foods: Acorns, other nuts, fruit, insects, bird eggs; sunflower and mixed seed at feeders.
Behaviors: Caches food for later use. Often harasses pets. Swoops into feeders, chasing off other birds.
Marks: Blue bird with crest, larger than a robin. White spots in wings and on tail edges. White or gray underparts; black necklace.
Voice: Harsh *"jeeah jeeah."* Imitates hawks.
Nests: Twigs and bark.
Confused with: Bluebirds are much smaller and lack crest; western scrub-jay lacks crest and white wing and tail spots.

Range: Regions 1 (Atlantic-Great Lakes), 2 (Southeast and South central), 3 (Mid and North Central), 4 (Northern Pacific and Rockies).

Steller's Jay
(Cyanocitta stelleri)

Size: Larger than robin, 13 inches (33 cm)
Habitat: Mostly mountain evergreen forests.
Foods: Omnivore; food includes insects, invertebrates, acorns, pine seeds, fruit; at feeders, sunflower seed and suet.
Behaviors: Caches and steals food from acorn woodpeckers.
Voice: Repeated, loud *"shack shack shack"* or *"shook shook shook."*
Marks: Dark bird with long, prominent crest. Brown-black head, breast, and back. Deep blue on wings, belly, rump, and tail.
Nests: Twigs, leaves, and mud; placed in shrub or tree.
Confused with: Blue jay shows white spots on wings and tail; western scrub-jay has no crest.
Range: Regions 4 (Northern Pacific and Rockies) and 5 (California and the Southwest.)
Factoid: Small groups of Stellar's jays patrol campsites looking for handouts.

Western Scrub-jay/Florida Scrub-jay
(Aphelocoma californica/A. coerulescens)

Note: Florida scrub-jay is now a separate species. Reports here are combined.

Size: Larger than robin, 12 inches (30.5 cm)

Habitat: Varied, including brush, desert scrub, orchards, canyons, suburbs.

Foods: Insects, acorns, bird eggs, frogs, berries; sunflower seed at feeders.

Behaviors: Long-term pair bonding, with pair remaining on feeding territory year round. Caches food, stealing frequently from acorn woodpeckers. Perches on deer to remove ticks.

Voice: Harsh *"check check check."* Also raspy *"kwesh, kwesh."*

Marks: Blue head, wings, tail; throat streaked, thin white eyebrow, gray back. In silhouette, the down-cocked tail is distinctive.

Nests: In shrubs.

Confused with: Distinct from Steller's jay, which has dark color, no white, and large crest. Gray jay has different habitat and has no blue coloring.

Range: Regions 2 (Southeast and South Central), 4 (Northern Pacific and Rockies), and 5 (California and the Southwest).

Gray Jay
(Perisoreus canadensis)

Size: Larger than robin, 12 inches (30.5 cm)

Habitat: Evergreen forests, open woodland, bogs.

Foods: Insects, fruit, carrion; peanuts and sunflower seed at feeders

Behaviors: Long-term pair bonding, with pair remaining on feeding territory year round. Caches food in saliva-permeated balls in trees. Tame, bold, and curious. Robs from campers. Nests early while snow is deep.

Voice: Soft *"whee-ah."*

Marks: Large gray bird with small black bill, black patch across back of neck, and white crown and face. Imagine an overgrown chickadee.

Nests: Bulky, well-woven nest of sticks and bark fastened with spider silk and insect cocoon, insulated with feathers, bark, and fur.

Confused with: Clark's nutcracker. Gray jay lacks black and white wings, white patches very obvious when nutcracker flies.

Range: Regions 1 (Atlantic-Great Lakes), 3 (Mid and North Central), 4

(Northern Pacific and Rockies), and 5 (California and the Southwest).

Northern Mockingbird
(Mimus polyglottos)

Size: Same size as robin, 10 inches (25 cm)

Habitat: Open areas with shrubs, gardens, parks.

Foods: Berries, insects, snails, small snakes, lizards; fruit at feeders.

Behaviors: Bully, charging after cats, hawks, squirrels, or snakes. Jerks wings up and over back to scare insects into moving.

Voice: Harsh, loud call, good mimic.

Marks: Overall gray above, lighter below, flashy white wing patches, long tail with white outer tail feathers.

Nests: Twigs, moss, leaves; in dense shrubs.

Confused with: Gray jay has shorter bill and Clark's nutcracker has no white eye line and a long pointed bill. Northern mockingbird has longer tail and more erect posture than either, and the white patches under wings are more central. Nutcracker wing white is on wing's back edge.

Factoid: The name comes from the bird's ability to imitate, including other birds' calls, whistles, squeaks, and suburban noises.

Range: All regions. Only the southern parts of Regions 3 and 4.

Brown-headed Cowbird
(Molothrus ater)

Size: Smaller than robin, 7 inches (18 cm)

Habitat: Pasture, lawns, forest clearings.

Foods: Insects, small fruit, seeds, small aquatic life; mixed seed on ground at feeders.

Behaviors: Gregarious bird, forms flocks of 50 to 200 birds. Feeds and roosts in enormous flocks with blackbirds and starlings in winter.

Marks: Females gray-brown overall with little distinct marking. Gray, cone-shaped beak. Males have distinctly brown heads and black glossy bodies with slight green iridescence.

Nests: Cowbirds lay their eggs in the nests of other birds, which raise the cowbird young.

Confused with: Blackbirds or sparrows, especially the female cowbirds. Blackbirds lack the distinctive brown heads of the males and have more pointed beaks. Sparrows are smaller

with more triangular beaks.
Range: All regions.

Hawks

Sharp-Shinned Hawk
(Accipiter striatus)
Size: Robin sized
to slightly larger,
10–14 inches
(25–35.5 cm)
Habitat: Woodland
hawk at home
in treed
neighborhoods.
Foods: Birds, some
small mammals,
frogs, lizards.
Behaviors: Bursts
from hiding
toward feeder to
snatch prey. Migrates in
large numbers.
Marks: Slim, small hawk with
matchstick slim yellow legs; broadly
banded, square-tipped tail; and short,
rounded wings. Hooked upper bill,
small lower bill to tear into prey. Dark
back, rusty-barred breast. Folded tail of
male is slightly notched or square.
Voice: High *"kik, kik, kik"* call.
Nests: Placed near trunk, broad flat
of sticks and twigs. Lined with
conifer needles.
Confused with: Male Cooper's hawks
and female sharp-shinned hawks can
be so similar that many cannot be
identified in the field. Sharp-shinned

hawks have wings pushed forward
at the wrist, and quick,
snappy wingbeats.
Range: All regions.

Cooper's Hawk
(Accipiter cooperii)
Size: Larger than a robin by up to 50
percent, 14–20 inches (35.5–51 cm)
Habitat: Woodland hawk.
Foods: Birds, some small mammals,
reptiles, amphibians.
Behaviors: Often stakes out bird
feeders. Secretive nester.
Marks: Very similar to sharp-shinned
hawk, but with pencil-sized legs. Short-
winged, long-tailed hawk. Tail is well
rounded even when folded.
Voice: *"Kek, kek, kek,"* lower than
sharp-shinned hawk, similar to the
call of a flicker around the nest.
Nests: Located near trunk or crotch
of trees, made of sticks and twigs.
Lined with chips and bark and
sometimes needles.
Confused with: Sharp-shinned hawk.
Cooper's hawks are larger and have
longer, rounder tail with a broader
white tip; adult has a square-headed
appearance as opposed to the sharp-
shinned hawk. Cooper's hawks have
stiff slow wingbeats and very straight
wings when compared to sharp-
shinned hawk.
Factoid: Hawk females are larger than
males. The difference in size can be up
to a third of the total.
Range: All regions.

Birds Seen Mostly on the Ground

American Robin
(Turdus migratorius)

Size: 10 inches (25 cm)
Habitat: Various. Lawns to mountains.
Foods: Earthworms, insects, berries; fruit at feeders.
Behaviors: Long, beautiful songs. Enthusiastic bather. Gathers in thickets or rows of bushes and trees.
Marks: Dark gray head and back, orange brown belly and breast, yellow bill. Female paler with same distribution of markings.
Nests: Grasses and mud, in tree or on building ledge.
Confused with: Varied thrush. Robin lacks distinctive orange line behind the eyes and orange wing bars.
Range: All regions.

Varied Thrush
(Ixoreus naevius)

Size: Slightly smaller than robin, 9.5 inches (24 cm)
Habitat: Moist evergreen woods.
Foods: Insects, earthworms, spiders, snails, seeds, berries; fruit or suet at feeders.
Behaviors: Prefers ground feeding in leaf litter.
Marks: Dark back and head, red-orange breast and belly with black or gray breast band. Orange line extending from above eye to back of neck on each side, orange wing bars.
Nests: Twigs and moss, on horizontal limb.
Confused with: American Robin. Robin has partial white-eye ring and lacks orange eye line and wing bars.
Range: Regions 4 (Northern Pacific and Rockies) and 5 (California and the Southwest).

Northern Flicker
(Colaptes auratus)

Size: Larger than robin, 13 inches (33 cm)
Habitat: Parks, suburbs, farms, woods.
Foods: Ants, insects, fruit; suet and seed at feeders.
Behaviors: Gobbles grubs on the ground, sometimes joining starlings and robins in this. Takes fruit from trees. In breeding season, it "drums" or pounds its bill on trees and dwellings. Courting males flash their wings to females.
Voice: Courtship call is *"wicka-wicka-wicka."* Call also runs down into a slurred sharp bark, *"keew, keew."*
Marks: Wide black necklace. Buffy breast with black spots; brown- and

Which Birds Visit Your Backyard?

As a family, you can discover which birds come to your backyard. Here's one fun afternoon project. Each person takes a piece of paper, makes drawings, and writes notes about one bird. Try to answer these questions about "your bird."

1. What was the bird doing when you saw it? (Did it feed on the ground or on the tube feeder? Did it peck at a tree?)
2. How large is the bird? (Is the bird bigger, smaller, or about the same size as a robin?)
3. What did you notice most about the bird? (Bright colors or dull? Any markings? Can you see the type of beak?)
4. Try to eliminate the categories that don't apply. Then think of which categories might your bird belong to.
- Birds That Cling to Trees: Mostly Woodpeckers
- Small Colorful Birds: Mostly Finches
- Medium to Large Black Birds and Jays
- Hawks
- Birds Seen Mostly on the Ground
5. Do you see any pictures in this chapter that look like your bird?
6. Keep your piece of paper. As you see your bird again, make more notes. You're a bird identification detective, and you need many clues to identify your suspect.

black-barred back and wings. In flight, flashy white rump patch. Males have "mustaches." In eastern birds, the mustache is black and the underside of wings show yellow. In western birds, the male mustache is red and underside of wings and tail show red.
Nests: Excavates in dead trees; may use existing hole or birdhouse.
Confused with: Distinctive. Not often confused.
Range: All regions.

Brown Thrasher
(Toxostoma rufum)

Size: Larger than robin, 11 1/2 inches (29 cm)
Habitat: Thickets and shrubs at edge of woods.
Foods: Insects, lizards, snakes, tree frogs, berries.
Behaviors: Uses long, strong bill to dig and sweep debris in food hunting.

Voice: Male has largest song list of any bird, more than 1,100 songs.
Marks: Bright brownish red or rufous above; heavy stripe on throat, breast, belly, and flanks. Slightly curved bill, long tail, and yellow eyes.
Nests: Twigs placed on ground or in vine tangle or dense shrubs.
Confused with: Thrushes and other thrashers. Brown thrashers have heavily

streaked breasts and light eyes.
Range: Regions 1 (Atlantic-Great
Lakes), 2 (Southeast and South Central),
3 (Mid and North Central), and 4
(Northern Pacific and Rockies).
Mainly east of the Rocky Mountains.

Carolina Wren
(Thryothorus ludovicianus)

Size: Smaller than robin, 5 1/2 inches
(13.3 cm)
Habitat: Wood edges, mountain forests,
aspen groves, suburbs.
Foods: Insects and spiders; suet
at feeders.
Behaviors: Energetic.
Voice: *"Tea-kettle, tea-kettle, tea-kettle."*
Beautiful singing voice.
Marks: Small brown bird about the size
of a sparrow. Warm red-brown on the
back, rump, and tail; buff below.
Eyebrow stripe is white and very
noticeable. Bird is stumpy and has
slender, slightly down-curved bill. Tail
is often cocked up.
Nests: Cavities made by other birds.
Confused with: Other wrens that are
smaller. Bewick's wren, with white eye
stripe, has white spots on tail edges
that distinguishes it from the
Carolina wren.

Range: Regions 1 (Atlantic-Great
Lakes), 2 (Southeast and South Central),
3 (Mid and North Central).

Dark-eyed Junco
(Junco hyemalis)

Slate-colored   Oregon

Size: Smaller than robin, 6 inches
(15 cm)
Habitat: Woods, bogs, mountains above
tree line, brush.
Foods: Seeds on ground and off trees;
mixed seed at feeders.
Behaviors: Travels in groups, visiting
feeders in winter. Prefers to feed on the
ground like sparrow relatives.
Overnights in brush piles.
Voice: Soft ticking.
Marks: Variable. Generally white
underparts, pale or white small bill.
Some forms have black hood and
brown back. Others are mostly gray.
Nests: Moss and grass, placed
on ground.
Confused with: Towhee's have similar
dark hoods, but also have distinctive
spotted wings (west) or white patch
on wings (east). Juncos are smaller than
towhees, and have a light colored beak,
rather than a dark one.
Range: All regions.

House Sparrow
(Passer domesticus)

male   female

Size: Smaller than a robin, 6 inches (15 cm)

Habitat: Prefer to live near people in urban or suburban areas or near farm buildings.

Foods: Spiders, insects including Japanese beetles, caterpillars, and aphids, seeds, and blossoms; seed or bread crumbs at feeders.

Behaviors: Travels in groups, chirping and squawking. In winter, roosts in large groups near people or in dense evergreens. Males hold their wings out and bow to court females.

Marks: Male has black bib, gray crown, cheek, breast. Female has brown crown, yellow bill, buffy eyebrow, and gray-brown breast.

Nests: Messy nest of string, grass, and cloth in crevice. Nesting locations stolen from bluebirds and swallows.

Confused with: Females look like many sparrows and finch females. Males are distinctive because of black bib and mask.

Factoid: This confusingly named bird is a weaver finch, not related to our domestic sparrow. House sparrows were introduced to the United States about 1850, and since have displaced many natives such as bluebirds, wrens, and other songbirds.

Range: All regions.

Song Sparrow
(Melospiza melodia)

Size: Smaller than robin, 6 inches (15 cm)

Habitat: Shrubs at edges of fields, lawns, and streams.

Foods: Insects, seeds, and some berries. Crustaceans and mollusks along coast. Corn, millet, hulled sunflower seed at ground feeders.

Behaviors: Flies low. Winter resident in many areas.

Marks: Streaked whitish breast, streaks sometimes merging into dark spot (similar to a stickpin) in center. Streaky brown above, brown wings, gray eyebrow. Prominent moustache. Rounded (not notched) tail.

Voice: Sings a complicated, varied warble year round. Starting with several short notes, the song has a long trill in the middle. The voice is slightly husky.

Nests: Grass cup on ground or shrub.

Confused with: Other sparrows.

Range: All regions.

Factoid: One of the most frequent cowbird nest hosts.

White-Crowned Sparrow
(Zonotrichia leucophrys)

Size: Smaller than robin, 7 inches (18 cm)
Habitat: Shrub borders, woods, gardens, parks.
Foods: Insects, seeds, other plants. Sometimes fly-catches; mixed seed on ground feeder.
Behaviors: Moves in mixed flocks of other sparrows.
Voice: One or two whistled notes followed by buzzy trills.
Marks: Mostly gray bird, no breast streaks. Clean black and white head stripes.
Nests: Grass, twigs, plant stems, on ground or shrub.
Confused with: White-throated sparrow, a browner, smaller bird with a clearly white throat patch; and golden-crowned sparrow, with golden yellow crown.
Range: All regions.

White-throated Sparrow
(Zonotrichia albicollis)

Size: Smaller than robin, 6 1/2 inches (16.5 cm)
Habitat: Lowland thickets.
Foods: Seeds, insects, berries.
Behaviors: Flocks with other sparrows, feeding on open ground; dives into cover. Feeds below bird feeders, scratching with both feet.
Voice: Males often sing at night. High whistles, *"Old Sam Peabody, Peabody, Peabody."*
Marks: Unstreaked gray breast, light and dark head stripes, bright white throat patch, buff back, rust-colored wings with white wing bars. Tan or white head stripes.
Nests: Clearing edge, of grasses, twigs, or pine needles lined with soft material
Confused with: White-crowned or golden-crowned sparrow.
Range: All regions.

Fox Sparrow
(Passerella iliaca)

Size: Smaller than robin, 6 1/4 inches (16 cm)
Habitat: Dense, brushy thickets.
Foods: Forages on ground for seeds, insects, some fruit.

Behaviors: In winter, joins other sparrows in mixed flocks. Adults give broken wing display to lure predators from the nest. Scratches back and forth in the underbrush when feeding.

Voice: Complex, melodious song.

Marks: Plain-faced sparrow with chevron-shaped spots on whitish breast and underparts. White eye ring, and brown to rufous upper parts.

Nests: Of grass, moss, root pieces, lined with soft materials, usually in thicket.

Confused with: Swainson's or hermit thrush, which are spotty rather than streaked or chevroned on the breast. Fox sparrow lacks the central breast spot of song sparrow, has a streaked breast that American tree sparrow lacks.

Range: All regions.

American Tree Sparrow,
(Spizella arborea)

Size: Smaller than robin, 6 1/4 inches (16.5 cm)

Habitat: Willow, scrub, brushy roadsides, weedy edges, marshes, feeders.

Foods: Spiders, insects, seeds, buds, willow and birch catkins, berries.

Scratch for millet beneath feeders.

Behaviors: Winters in northern United States and very southern edge of Canada. Breeds in Alaska and northern Canada. Bathes in water. Eats snow. Roosts alone in shelters on ground or in evergreens.

Voice: Sweet song, one or two high clear notes at beginning.

Marks: Clear-breasted sparrow with single dark spot on breast and solid red-brown cap. Dark upper bill, light below. Two white wing bars.

Nests: Cup-shaped nest in grass hummock. Made of grass and bark lined with feathers or fur.

Confused with: Lacks streaked breast of fox sparrow and song sparrow. Distinctive from field sparrow by uniformly colored bill.

Range: All regions.

Chipping Sparrow
(Spizella passerina)

Size: Smaller than robin, 5 1/4 inches (13.3 cm)

Habitat: Open woods, evergreens, orchards, farms, towns.

Foods: Insects, spiders, seeds. Scratch for millet beneath feeders.

Behaviors: Wanders in family groups. In winter, forages in flocks of 25 to 50 birds with juncos and field sparrows.

Voice: A rattle on one pitch.

Marks: Clear-breasted, gray sparrow with brown-red cap, white eyebrow, and black line through the eye. Wings and back streaked.

Nests: Cup-shaped nests in vine tangles of grass and lined with hair or fur.

Confused with: Unstreaked white underside and black eye line clear through eye to bill distinguishes the chipping sparrow from other sparrows.

Range: All regions.

Factoid: Can survive on dry seeds without drinking water for 3 weeks.

Eastern/Spotted Towhee
(Pipilo erythrophthalmus/P. maculatus)

Note: For the purposes of data reporting, Project FeederWatch treats these two species as one.

Size: Smaller than robin, 8 inches (20 cm)

Habitat: Open woods with shrubs.

Foods: Insects, spiders, lizards, seeds, berries; mixed seed at feeders. Prefers ground feeding.

Behaviors: Searches through leaf litter, jumping forward and scratching back to find insects. Rarely sits still. Solitary, prefers rows of trees or bushes for perching.

Voice: Eastern towhee calls, *"drink your tea."* Eastern and spotted towhees make a buzzy, guttural *"Toe-WHEET"* call.

Marks: Black hood, back, wings. Orange flanks, white belly. White wing spots. Orange eyes. Females, brown hood. White corners of tail are distinctive.

Nests: Large collection of twigs placed on or near ground.

Confused with: Dark-eyed junco. Distinguished by towhee's distinctive spotted wings (west) or white patch on wings (east). Juncos are smaller than Towhees, and have a light-colored beak, rather than a dark one.

Range: All regions.

Factoid: The bird's name comes from the call, *"Toe-WHEET."*

Mourning Dove
(Zenaida macroura)

Size: Larger than robin, 12 inches (30.5 cm)

Habitat: Any open habitat, including suburbs.

Foods: Seeds and some insects; mixed seed on ground or low platform feeders.

Behaviors: Males bow and lift their heads and coo repeatedly when defending their territories. Pairs usually nest several times each year. Males incubate during the day, females at night.

Marks: Gray-brown slim, pigeonlike bird. Long pointed tail and black dots on wings.

Voice: Mournful *"cooah coo coo,"* often mistaken by new birders for an owl. When doves fly, their wings make a whistling sound.

Nests: Made of loose twigs; supported by tree, shrub, or ledge, 3–30 feet (1–9 m) high.

Confused with: Rock pigeons. Distinguished by dove's slim profile, long tail, and consistent soft color.

Range: All regions.

Rock Pigeon
(Columba livia)

Size: Larger than robin, 13 inches (33 cm)

Habitat: Cities, parks, buildings, and bridges.

Foods: Seeds and waste grain; at feeders, mixed seed on ground.

Behaviors: Walks on ground, head bobs forward with feet.

Voice: Gurgled *"coo-roo-coo."*

Marks: Heavy-bodied bird. Red eyes and feet, normal gray back, and iridescent neck, but color varies widely. The common city pigeon.

Nests: Roots, stems, and leaves; on building ledges and bridge beams.

Confused with: Mourning dove; the rock pigeon has stout body, square tail, and iridescence over multicolored body.

Range: All regions.

Watching birds is fun for the whole family.

Chapter 4

Enjoying Your

Backyard Birds

In the bird world, feather care, migration, breeding, and feeding are the key activities. Knowing a bit about each of the life-and-death issues of backyard birds increases your appreciation of things you never imagined you'd see outside your window. This chapter is your kick-start to learning bird behavior basics.

How to See the Birds

When you want to observe the general behavior of a bird or a flock of birds, the best way to start is with your unaided eyes. Looking unaided allows you to see the full range of the birds' activities—the "whole picture" of the bird's response to what is going on in his world. You can't see this through binoculars. Then, when you want to see details, use a pair of binoculars.

Choosing a Pair of Binoculars

Binocular selection can be a complicated subject. The many options and features available in today's optics can be overwhelming. Some of these features may become important if you decide to pursue bird watching seriously. However, there's no need for your first selection of binoculars to be an anxiety-producing experience. Beginner observer criteria are not complicated.

Start your binoculars search at one of the stores that specialize in backyard bird-related feed and supplies. Binoculars made for birding have a relatively close focus and quality lenses for detail. Try several brands. Use the same "targets," one 8 feet (2.5 m) away, and another 25 yards (23 m) away. Purchase the pair you prefer. For those who wear eyeglasses, binoculars should have fold-down rubber eye rings and a good width of field. Nothing is more frustrating that having a poor experience with your first pair of binoculars.

An excellent choice of binoculars is either a "7 x 35" or an "8 x 42" pair of binoculars. Although models can range in price from the very inexpensive to costly, a pair of binoculars from the mid-lower end of the price scale can serve you well for many years. Shopping for a good used pair can be an excellent idea, but make sure that used binoculars are in alignment. Many birders start with a good beginner pair and sell them as they move to more expensive binoculars that give them a more finely detailed view. Because this is an important purchase, stores that specialize in bird supplies and optics are an excellent source of the information you need when beginning your bird-watching hobby.

Using Your Eyes to Identify

Use your eyes to identify the bird. What is the bird doing? Where is it? Is the bird larger or smaller than a robin (which is a 10-inch [25-cm] bird)? What do you notice most about the bird's appearance? With the answers to these questions, you can identify the birds in this book much more easily.

Binoculars provide a detailed view of your backyard birds and their behaviors.

What Do the Binocular Numbers Mean?

Binoculars are identified by two numbers, as in "7 x 35" or "8 x 42." The first number is the magnification or power. In the case of "7 x 35," the 7 means the image appears through the binoculars seven times as large as with your unaided eye. Many people do not understand that more magnification is not always better. At higher magnification, the slightest arm movement blurs the image. Sometimes higher magnification means less clarity. Much backyard birding is done at close range. You want a pair of binoculars that focuses at close range. A 10-foot (3-m) close focus is not acceptable. You want to be able to focus on birds 6 to 8 feet (1.8 to 2.4 m) away.

The binoculars' second number indicates the light that enters the lens. The most common number is 35. Next is 40, which gathers more light. Aim for a 35 or 40 binocular. Ultralight binoculars sacrifice light-gathering ability but weigh less. Ultralight binoculars are great for viewing in high light, but are not good for viewing in the early morning or late afternoon, or for looking at a wren under the shadows of a bush.

Feather Basics and Feather Care

Feathers, used for temperature control and flight, are the most distinctive characteristic of a bird's anatomy. A bird has a set of 2,000 to 3,000 feathers. A healthy bird cleans, lubricates, and returns each feather to its special position each day, in the same way that pilots check an aircraft each time it flies. Feathers have to be in good condition for flying.

Types of Feathers

The feathers that cover a bird's body are contour feathers. Underneath are the down feathers that provide insulation. Contour and down feathers provide temperature control.

FAMILY-FRIENDLY TIP

The "How To Use Binoculars" Game

The key to using binoculars effectively is practice. The whole family can work together on this. You'll need paper or cardboard, a magic marker, a long tape measure, and a tack.

Each member of the family, using a dark colored magic marker, writes the name of a bird on a piece of cardboard or paper. Make the word the size of a robin. (10 inches [25 cm] long and 5 inches [13 cm] tall.) Keep your word secret. The youngest person goes first. Take your word to a place 16 feet away from a starting point. Tack your word to a tree or bush.

Each person finds the sign with his eyes and, without moving his head, brings the binoculars up to his eyes. What bird name do you see? Keep it to yourself. When the family is finished, compare notes. Who was able to focus on the bird name? Was everyone able to get the word?

Repeat, using measurements of 8, 20, and 40 feet (2.5, 6, and 12 m). Help each other until everyone has had a turn and everyone knows how to find the words.

For the next round of the game, make the word smaller. Focus your eyes on the smaller word. Then bring the binoculars up to your eyes. When you can do this consistently with the bird name, you're ready for the real, moving birds.

Always, always, always, use your eyes first.

Flight feathers, those attached to the wing, are of two types: primary and secondary. The primary feathers are those you see when the bird is at rest. The secondary feathers can more easily be seen when the bird opens his wings for flight.

Because the feathers have different jobs, their structure is different. Contour feathers are almost circular and cover the body and the downy plumes. The contour feathers cover the entire body, lying flat, to give the bird speed as well as warmth. Think of the clothing cyclists wear in a race. Primary

Tail feather of a blue jay. Feathers found on the ground are usually primaries, secondaries, or tail feathers.

and secondary feathers are the long thin ones you find on the ground. They have a central rib and small plumes that "zip" together to form a continuous surface. This continuous surface gives the bird a smooth wing, similar to an airplane wing.

Color

Color is one aspect of feathers. Birds display a wide diversity of plumage colors and patterns. Birds use color to increase conspicuousness during breeding season, as when a mockingbird fans his tail and raises his wings, flashing a bright color contrasting with his body. Attraction of mates is an important use of feathers.

In many bird species, the males are more brightly colored than are the females. In others, color variation between male and female is indistinguishable. Some males and females of a species look so dissimilar that the first observers thought these birds were of different species.

Birds also use their color to hide from predators. A flock of 50 brightly colored goldfinches can disappear into a tree, leaving first-time watchers slack-jawed in disbelief. The colorful nature of birds' feathers is enhanced by light. As birds disappear into the interior of the tree, away from the sunlight, they appear to be dark colored, like the interior leaves of the tree.

Preening

Preening is one aspect of feather care. Birds stroke their feathers, pulling them through their bills. Preening helps the feathers lie flatly, so they are less likely

Male and Female: Similar, Identical, or Different?

Male and female feather patterns and colors can look so different that the two sexes can appear to be different bird species. Sometimes male and female feather patterns and colors are so identical that only a close examination by an expert might distinguish the two sexes. Similar-looking males and females may have a coloring that is only slightly different, either in pattern or in the intensity of the colors. This table identifies which common species have different, similar, or identical-looking sexes.

Sexes Different	Sexes Similar	Sexes Identical
American Goldfinch	American Robin	American Crow
Brown-headed Cowbird	Common Grackle	American Tree Sparrow
Evening Grosbeak	Common Redpoll	Chipping Sparrow
House Finch	Dark-eyed Junco	Black-capped/ Carolina Chickadee
House Sparrow	Downy Woodpecker	Blue Jay
Lesser Goldfinch	Eastern/Spotted Towhee	Brown Thrasher
Northern Cardinal	Hairy Wookpecker	Carolina Wren
Pine Grosbeak	Northern Flicker	Chestnut-backed Chickadee
Purple Finch	Pileated Woodpecker	Common Raven
Red-winged Blackbird	Pine Siskin	Cooper's hawk
	Red-bellied Woodpecker	European Starling
	Red-breasted Nuthatch	Fox Sparrow
	Varied Thrush	Gray Jay
	White-breasted Nuthatch	Mountain Chickadee
	Yellow-rumped Warbler	Mourning Dove
		Northern Mockingbird
		Rock Pigeon
		Ruby-crowned Kinglet
		Sharp-shinned Hawk
		Song Sparrow
		Steller's Jay
		Tufted Titmouse
		Western Scrub-Jay
		White-crowned Sparrow
		White-throated Sparrow

Birds will use water features for both drinking and bathing.

to be broken, and smoothly, so that they produce better aerodynamics and insulation. Birds preen every feather each day, applying oil from the preen gland at the base of the tail to keep feathers flexible and in good condition. Feather condition is also enhanced when sunlight helps break down old and spread new oil, reduce bacteria, and expose parasites for removal.

Bathing

Bathing is important for feather maintenance. After bathing, birds preen to remove the remainder of the plant juices and dirt that feathers pick up during the bird's daily activities and night roost. Different birds have different bathing types. Woodland birds bathe by dousing themselves in puddles or perching out in the mist or rain. Drier-habitat birds use a bathing

variation, using the dew on leaves or grass as a substitute for a pool of water. Still other birds perch out in the open so that mist soaks their feathers. (Oddly, birds also bathe in dusty spots on the ground, to kill mites.) In birdbaths, birds stroll into shallow water, squat breast deep, and scoop water onto their backs with their wings.

The opportunity to drink and bathe will bring birds to your yard. You can present water in a variety of ways, including standing water, or moving water in the form of a misting or dripping system.

Feeding Details

Bird digestion is adapted for their special energy requirements and their lack of teeth and saliva. Birds maintain high body temperatures (ranging from

104°F to 112°F [40°C to 44.4°C] compared to 98.6°F [37 °C]for people). Also, flight is an energy-intensive activity. As a result, small birds eat about 20 percent of their body weight each day. This is like a 150-pound (68-kg) person eating 30 pounds (13.6 kg) of food every day!

The bird's liver provides quick access to carbohydrates. Keeping the food supply constant is the role of the bird's crop. The crop is a large pouch in the esophagus where food collects when a bird feeds. As digestion occurs and the bird uses energy, more food drops from the crop to the "stomach." Think reservoir.

A bird's "stomach" has two parts. One applies digestive juices. The other, the gizzard, grinds. The gizzard functions for the bird like our molars do. Birds that swallow seeds whole use grit, particles of dirt or stone that they swallow, to grind whole seed. Doves and pigeons are examples of birds that swallow seeds whole.

Flocking

Flocking is a survival strategy for birds. The security of a large group enables an individual to relax its personal vigil for predators and hence to feed more deliberately. One reason this works is that predator detection improves when many eyes are vigilant, resulting in greater individual security for all flock members. In addition, predators have difficulty focusing on one bird when many flush; the flock movement is confusing. Flocks also are better at spotting feeding opportunities.

Birds flush together at the approach of a predator because individuals synchronize their takeoffs with a series of flight intention movements that prime every bird's readiness for flight. Finally, by calling loudly, potential victims rob a predator of the element of surprise, reducing the likelihood of attack.

In fall and winter, some bird species travel in what are called mixed flocks. These flocks are temporary alliances of several different species of birds that

Tufted titmice will form mixed species flocks with other small birds.

feed together in an area. This arrangement gives birds that are not part of a flock the advantages of protection and help in identifying likely food sources.

Rhythm of the Day

Light helps establish the rhythm of a bird's days. Birds become active just as dawn occurs, singing and calling to create what is known as the dawn chorus. This is how birds reconnect with each other. Birds leave the roost in the morning to forage. They sleep or preen quietly at midday, and have several hours of active foraging and socializing before roosting again at dusk. Calling and singing has to do with attracting mates, defending territory, and maintaining social order.

Songs advertise a male with a territory looking for a female, similar to a personals ad: "Single male with good job seeks female for marriage and children." Most of our backyard birds sing. Hawks are an exception. Thrushes are excellent singers.

Calls are about communication of a type other than courtship. American goldfinches, for example, make their *"per-chik-o-ree"* call as they fly. This keeps the birds together, in contact with one another. Birds also use calls to signal threats, as distress or alarm signals, or to request food. If you've had nesting birds in your yard, you know that when a parent arrives at the nest, the begging calls from the nestlings are persistent.

More About Bird Food

The profiles in Chapter 3 show that birds eat many things that humans wouldn't care for: road kill, spiders, weed seeds. Birds' diets are generally repetitive; many of the same foods are taken repeatedly. During the breeding season and during molting, this changes.

The amino acids needed to build protein come only from other protein. Omnivores, like blackbirds, eat as much insect protein as possible. Sparrows, mostly seed eaters, increase their insect eating to feed their young during the breeding season, using the carbohydrates from the seeds for their own energy requirements

Adults feed baby birds massive quantities of protein to help them grow and develop rapidly. Even hummingbirds, which we might think of as exclusively nectar-drinking birds, catch insects for protein to balance their diet.

During the day, you'll notice an order to the procession of birds through your yard. In a given season, the order will be relatively stable, with the same birds visiting at about the same times each day.

Seasonal Rhythms

Aside from establishing the rhythm of daily behavior, light provides cues regarding seasonal behaviors. The effect of light on hormone production triggers molting, courtship, breeding, and migration. The hormones affect birds' bodies and minds.

Fall

Seasonal feeding patterns are consistent from year to year. In fact, many feeder watchers mark the seasons' passing by the arrival of particular birds. Often accurate within a day or two, a record of the first occurrence of goldfinches or grosbeaks marks the beginning of fall. Some feeder watchers associate the leaves changing color with the arrival of sparrows and juncos. Which birds arrive depends on your geography and the cover and food your yard offers.

Birds migrate to survive, and fall migration is about finding food and a secure habitat for the winter months. Birds that overwinter in your area move in during fall. Birds migrating from north to south may also stop in your yard along their route to feed for a few days. Most birds switch from insects to seed to provide extra energy for the trip.

Migratory birds visit feeders in the fall on the way to their winter ranges.

Migration patterns vary from long-distance migration, as in the case of hummingbirds that migrate from Canada to South America, to shorter migration, such as moving from Alaska to Minnesota, to no migration, as in the case of the black-capped chickadee, which stays in the same place year round. Some birds migrate from higher elevations to lower elevations within the same regions because the food sources at the higher elevations are not available during colder weather

With each fall week, the numbers of each bird type at your feeder will rise and fall as migrants arrive and depart. The birds in your backyard may look different for another reason: For many songbirds, fall feather appearance is different from that seen in spring. Also, birds that hatched over the summer will still have their immature feather patterns, even though they travel with the adults.

A special treat occurs at night, when many migrating birds move. Open your windows to hear the calls overhead. As the sun rises, birds come down to find food and cover in which to rest during the day.

Winter

During the winter, birds can be welcome sights amid storms and gray days. Suet becomes more popular in winter, as do the "gone to seed" flowers, weeds, and berry bushes. Ground feeders scratch through the leaves and mulch for seed. Birds work their established feeding territories in fairly predictable patterns, with many birds foraging together in multi-species, mixed flocks.

If you live in a place without snow, check out the Feeder-cam at Cornell in Ithaca, where there's usually plenty of snow. You'll see more mixed-flock foraging and learn more about the temporary alliances that birds form. See the Resources section for the web site or use a search engine.

Spring

In spring, migrants moving north may stop at your feeder again. Birds resident in your area begin to set up territories. Their feathers brighten as many molt into breeding plumage. You begin to see courtship behavior. Mating pairs build nests. Eggs hatch, and the pair begins the process of rearing their young.

In spring, hormones induced by the seasonal variations in hours of daylight, stimulate molting, usually the prelude to courtship and breeding.

The Expert Knows

Signs of Courtship

Birds communicate with each other using body postures called displays. In your backyard, you'll see displays in high numbers in the spring. Birds beg, greet, and show aggression using predictable body postures.

Courtship displays often showcase a male's striking plumage, as when the red-winged blackbird puffs up its wing patch or the rock pigeon spreads its tail. Some birds lower their bills. Others vibrate their wings, fluff their body feathers, raise their bills, and push their bills forward as they take rapid small steps.

Molting

During the molt, a bird replaces his entire set of feathers. Birds producing feathers during molting replace up to 10 percent of their body mass. This process requires lots of nutrition. Molting is the first step in a progression of behavior that includes courtship, breeding, and nesting.

Courtship

Courtship in birds begins with shiny new feathers to impress a mate. Males typically stake out territories and begin to sing, becoming more aggressive at feeders—and everywhere else—as they compete for the attention of females.

In addition to singing, males position themselves to show their brilliant new feathers, often strutting, raising their crests, spreading their tail feathers, or flashing their wing patches. Females select males on the basis of their territory defense and on the basis of their feathers.

In spring, sparrows arrive. Cardinals begin to look for mates early in the season. The goldfinches' plumage begins to show blotches of bright yellow. In a process that lasts for several weeks, the new feathers replace old ones worn from migration

and use. The males of the species begin to sing and display.

The tempo at your feeder may increase, with most male birds showing signs of aggression toward others of their species.

This is an excellent time of year to stay committed to feeding. For example, American robins return to their breeding places at the first sign of spring, but often they arrive before the last snowfall. With their natural food buried under snow, they could use fruit and raisins to help them through until the snow melts. They'll complete their molt and begin courtship—an exhausting and nutritionally demanding time.

Nesting

Once birds have selected mates, the next step is creating the nest. Some

Singing is part of the courtship behavior of many backyard birds, such as house wrens.

Eggs

Eggs are perfect development chambers for birds. Oxygen comes through the shell, carbon dioxide and water vapor move out, and the parent birds provide the warmth necessary for development. Inside, the yolk provides energy for growth.

Small birds lay proportionately larger eggs: A wren's egg is 13 percent of the wren's weight, whereas an ostrich egg is 2 percent of the adult's weight. Streamlined birds like hummingbirds lay elliptical eggs. Owls' eggs are nearly round.

Egg color and shell thickness varies enormously. In most bird species, the colors of eggs help with their camouflage, although this leaves no explanation for the blue eggs of robins.

Most songbirds do not incubate their eggs until all are laid. Incubating the eggs begins their development to hatching. This explains why most songbird eggs hatch within a few hours of each other.

watchers are as fascinated by nest construction as by any other aspect of bird behavior. You can answer many questions through patient observation from the comfort of your home. What materials do Carolina wrens use in building nests? Exactly where is the nest? Are both parents building the nest?

Many backyard bird watchers love to attract birds to their yards by supplying nesting opportunities. Finding out what it will take to entice a particular bird to nest in your yard can become quite competitive. Not only can you attract birds to nest in your yard, but also birds that nest elsewhere can gather materials from your yard. The selection process itself is fascinating.

Factors in the nesting equation include a place to nest and the building materials for the outer construction and inner lining of the nests.

Summer

In summer, the baby birds are being fed and fledged from the nest, in a gradual process that involves a period of independence. The parents are exhausted from their efforts to rear the young, teach their youngsters to fly, and feed themselves. Young continue to beg, and the parents continue to feed their young, but they typically make the youngster fly in order to be rewarded with food.

Early flight training can be comical to watch, but the purpose is important. Within a few weeks, birds that migrate will be leaving the summer breeding and feeding grounds to make the journey to their overwintering

Baby Birds

Some baby birds are capable of leaving the nest on the day of hatching. Ducklings and grouse chicks are examples. But all songbirds are naked, blind, and helpless on hatching.

Just-hatched songbirds must be kept warm until their feathers develop and allow the young to leave the nest. Their eyes open well in advance of this, but the baby birds are defenseless. The parents find food for themselves and their young, who are dependent on concealment in the nest for protection from predators.

When feathers have developed, the young leave the nest. Now called fledglings, they spend time on the ground learning to walk and fly. During this time, parents continue to feed the fledgling. (Don't pick them up. The parents are caring for them during this normal transition time.)

This is an excellent time to keep your pets indoors. Within a week, the fledglings will be able to fly from danger.

territory. In some species, the adult birds migrate first, leaving the young behind to bulk up and mature before making their first migration.

Feather colors fade as fall approaches. Some birds undergo a molt, making them less conspicuous before moving to their new location.

Strange Behaviors

By bringing wild birds into your more-or-less civilized backyard, you have invited the birds to bring their entire repertoire of behaviors with them. Some of these behaviors may appear strange to you, but there is a reason for all of them.

Pecking on Glass

During the breeding season, wildlife care centers receive many calls. Pecking on glass or mirrors is a frequent one. In most cases, the bird is a male that sees his reflection in the glass or mirror. He believes he sees an intruder in his territory. Pecking is his attack on "the other bird." You can resolve the problem by eliminating the reflection. Try drawing the curtains or putting a sticky note on the window. You and your territorial backyard bird will experience tension relief.

Drumming on the House

The breeding season is also the time when some birds drum on the house. Typically, the bird is a flicker, and the drumming is on flashing around the chimney or on any other part of the structure that makes a big noise. The drumming announces his territory, and is part of his advertisement for a mate.

The good news is that the season is relatively short. To discourage drumming birds, try to cover any vulnerable areas being hammered.

More good news is that the nest site is probably nearby. Look for it by watching the flicker carefully.

Mobbing

Mobbing occurs when one species of bird tries to drive off another. Mobbing is an easy way to find hawks (raptors), which are usually the object of the mobbing. Very noticeable with crows, but done by many species of birds including blackbirds, a crowd of the smaller species, making full alarm call cries, flies at the intruder, who has settled too near a roost or a nest, or is attacking a nest. The mobbing creates a ruckus that can be heard throughout the neighborhood. Usually, the predator flies off, and the smaller birds pursue in a short chase.

Birds on the Ground

During the spring and summer, people become concerned when they see birds on the ground. Normally, these are perfectly healthy fledglings. All flighted birds spend time on the ground being looked after by their parents while they improve their walking and flying skills. If you see a bird on the ground calling, it's calling to its parent to come and feed it. Leave the bird where it is, and retreat out of sight. The parent will not feed the bird while you are watching.

Crows and other birds will mob raptors, such as the kestrel.

Chapter 5

Backyard Bird

Activities

You have looked at the groups of birds in your area and worked with a basic backyard food and water setup. You've explored your top local feeder birds in more detail and learned more about their behavior. Now you're ready to have more fun. When you know the birds you want to attract, you know what habitat to supply. When you know habitat, you can create it. Food, water, shelter, and a place to rear young makes habitat that will fill with birds. The more combinations you have, the more birds (and other wild things) will reside near your home.

This chapter introduces your family to many different types of activities, including experimenting with feeders and water sources, keeping notes on your birds' activities, connecting with people of similar interests, and trying seasonal kids' activities that involve backyard birds.

Experimenting With Feeders

Feeders come in many styles to dispense different types of foods: suet, nut, corn, fruit, and peanut butter. Feeder designs, such as tray or platform feeders or tube feeders, accommodate certain types of birds and their feeding habits and discourage others. Feeder designs also exclude certain animals. Hoppers, squirrel-proof caged feeders, and hanging plastic spheres all exclude large birds. Finally, feeders such as the stick-on window feeder accommodate specific homeowner circumstances.

Most backyard bird lovers develop their feeding station setup to attract those groups of birds they appreciate most while minimizing the birds or other animals they find less desirable.

Platform Feeders

Platform feeders are square or rectangular surfaces with a raised lip to keep the seed inside the feeder. These feeders provide free access for birds and maximum viewing for the watcher. They can hold large seeds, fruit, or mealworms. They are often mounted on a pole or hung from a wire, but you can also find platform feeders with short legs to use as ground feeders.

The disadvantage of platform feeders is the potential for domination by large birds or squirrels. Another problem is that, because the seed is unprotected, rain or snow can turn the seed to mush, and wind can scatter the seed.

Low platform feeders will attract ground-feeding birds, such as mourning doves.

A quality platform feeder has a strong wire mesh bottom to allow water to drain and make cleaning the feeder easier.

Suet attracts many birds, including woodpeckers, nuthatches, and catbirds.

Hopper Feeders

Hopper feeders add a roof and seed reservoir to the basic platform design. Like the platform feeder, hoppers are usually mounted on a pole or hung from a wire. The seed reservoir and roof make them easier to maintain. The disadvantage is the higher cost of the initial purchase.

A well-constructed hopper is sturdy and provides metal screen feeding surfaces or other means for water to drain from the seeds on the landing and feeding areas.

Some hopper feeders are weighted feeders; heavier birds, such as starlings, landing on the perch, shut the feeder. Smaller birds on the perch do not close the feeder.

Tube Feeders

Tube feeders, such as our starter feeder, are usually made of heavy-duty plastic with openings designed for a particular type of seed and perches near each of the openings to accommodate small, agile birds. These feeders are easy to hang and maintain.

The features of a quality feeder include sturdy materials, a well-designed cap to keep water away from the seed, and a means to prevent seed

from remaining at the bottom of the tube.

Modified tube feeders include the thistle feeder. Thistle feeders house the Nyjer thistle seed that small acrobatic birds prefer. They have tiny holes for the birds to access the seed and many perches.

Peanut meat feeders are another variation on the tube feeder. The tube is made of sturdy wire mesh, with openings large enough for chickadees and nuthatches; it will attract these small clinging birds.

Suet Feeders

Feed suet, the fat that surrounds beef kidneys, from a rubber- or plastic-coated wire mesh box affixed to a hardwood tree trunk. Wire mesh, box-shaped suet feeders can be hung from a wire or mounted on a pole with good results. A variation of the wire mesh suet feeder adds a board extending about 4-6 inches (10-15 cm) below the feeder. This "tail prop" board allows feeding woodpeckers to prop their tails against the board as they would against the trunk of a tree.

Suet feeders are inexpensive, and the steady stream of chickadees, jays, nuthatches, titmice, and woodpeckers they attract will keep you busy observing.

Suet is available in prepackaged slabs to fit the wire mesh feeders. You can also purchase suet from your local meat counter.

Nectar Feeders

Nectar feeders accommodate hummingbirds and other lovers of sweet sap. These feeders hold a solution of sugar and water that birds sip through openings in the base of the feeder, near the perches. Nectar feeders attract orioles, woodpeckers, sapsuckers, cardinals, chickadees, finches, warblers, and grosbeaks in addition to hummingbirds.

Some hummingbird feeders come with "bee guards." Removing the bee guards can provide access to birds with beaks larger than those of hummingbirds and warblers.

A solution of 4 parts water to 1 part white table sugar works well for hummingbirds. To mix in 2-cup batches, use a 1/2-cup of sugar and 2 cups of water. Stir. Table sugar requires boiling water to dissolve completely. Superfine sugar works in cold water.

Birds such as orioles prefer a solution of 5 parts water to 1 part table sugar.

Books by Writers Who Observed Backyard Birds

Rare Encounters with Ordinary Birds: Notes from a Northwest Year, by Lyanda Lynn Haupt. Seattle: Sasquatch Books, 2001.

Why I Wake Early: New Poems, by Mary Oliver. Boston: Beacon Press, 2004.

Songs to Birds: Essays, by Jake Page. Boston: D. R. Godine, 1993.

Refuge: An Unnatural History of Family and Place, by Terry Tempest Williams. New York: Vintage Books, 2001.

Red-Tails in Love: A Wildlife Drama in Central Park, by Marie Winn. Updated ed. New York: Vintage Departures, 2005.

Never use honey, which birds cannot digest, or artificial sweetener, which robs birds of necessary calories. Red dye in the nectar is unnecessary. A small touch of red on the feeder is enough to attract most birds.

It is important to clean nectar feeders each time you refill them, so select one for easy cleaning. In warm weather, the solution spoils quickly. You'll need to clean the nectar feeder every 2 or 3 days, whether the nectar is used up or not.

The horizontal or shallow bowl-shaped feeders are easy to wash with a sponge. The tall glass feeders require a bottle brush. Use glass or clear feeders so that you can see when the food level is low.

Other Feeder Types

Veteran bird-feeding enthusiasts insist that you can attract warblers—small, very colorful birds not usually seen at feeders. One popular method, in addition to nectar feeders, is a peanut butter stick. Make this feeder using a 6-inch (15-cm) piece of wood or a stick. Drill small holes into the wood. Pack the holes with peanut butter, and hang the stick outside in a place near cover. Start by placing your new feeder near a shrub that you know a warbler favors.

Feeder Mounts

As you add feeders, you will need to consider feeder mounts. What is adequate for a small beginning feeder doesn't translate as you create a backyard feeding station. How a feeder is mounted plays an important part in your success and in the convenience of your set up.

Shepherd's crook poles are easy to use. You just step on the anchoring foot to secure the pole in the ground. Shepherd's crook poles come in single and multi-arm versions. Similar-style poles that mount on deck railings also are available.

These mounts are attractive, easy to install, and easy to move if you've placed the feeder in a less than ideal place. The drawback is that, if the feeder gets a lot of traffic, the mounts may not be able to carry the weight.

Posts made from rot-resistant wood can carry lots of weight and look nice with plantings. Wood posts should be set in a hole 12 to 15 inches (30.5-38 cm) deep for a 3- to 4-foot (about 1 m) post. Gravel at the foot of the hole creates drainage and ensures that the post will last longer.

Steel posts made from sections that slide together provide a modern look. Painted black, these straight poles blend in to any landscaping scheme

Nectar feeders are the only type of feeder that will attract hummingbirds. This is an Anna's hummingbird.

and can be installed using the same method as with a wooden post, or they can be placed in a patio-style umbrella-stand mount. Be sure to purchase a collar or flange for the top of the pole for easy feeder attachment.

Nyjer seed attracts goldfinches, purple finches, and siskins.

More About Food Types

As you increase the number of feeders and learn more about the birds you want to attract, seed selection becomes a tool you can use to manage your budget, the maintenance of seed waste, and the bird traffic at your feeders.

Birdseed is a mixture of grains and seeds. To make best use of your dollars, you must know which birds prefer which seeds. Be wary of purchasing seed mixes. Corn, wheat, milo, or sorghum mixed into your sunflower creates a lower amount of the seeds that your most desired birds will eat.

Waste-free seed mixes, such as hulled seed, are an alternative to consider. Although these seeds are more expensive, they have the advantage of being entirely edible. This means less waste, less cleanup, and less mess around the base of your feeder.

Sunflower Seed

Sunflower seed is a staple that satisfies more than 20 types of feeder birds. The large-beaked seed eaters, such as cardinals, grosbeaks, and jays, prefer

this seed. Chickadees, finches, nuthatches, and other smaller-beaked birds also use sunflower seed as a staple. Sunflower seed takes care of most fall and winter feeder birds except for sparrows.

It comes in two types: striped and black oil. The more economical black-oil sunflower seed has more pieces per pound than the striped variety. Also, smaller birds can crack it more easily.

Black-oil sunflower is a small seed with high energy content and thin shells. This seed is a favorite of cardinals, finches, and a wide variety of other birds. Striped sunflower seeds are larger and have a thicker shell. Birds with larger bills can crack these shells.

Millet

White or proso millet is a small, round seed. Millet is a lightweight seed, so you get many seeds per pound. Doves, juncos, quail, towhees, and sparrows—all ground foraging birds—prefer millet.

Do not confuse millet with milo. Milo is a reddish round grain, a component of inexpensive seed mixes. Most birds do not appreciate milo, making milo a seed that collects under the feeder and causes problems, rather than bringing delight to you or your backyard birds.

Nyjer

Nyjer, a seed that attracts finches like goldfinches, purple finches, and siskins, also goes by the name *thistle seed*. The name is misleading. This is not the seed of common North American thistle species, most of which are invasive plants.

More expensive than most seed, a little of this imported seed goes a long way, especially if you dispense it from a high-quality feeder with heavy metal fastenings to ensure that the feeder does not release seed in the wind or rain. Nyjer is a favorite food of the finch family, including American goldfinches, pine siskins, and common redpolls.

To ensure that your Nyjer seed is not wasted, purchase tube feeders with perches above the seed holes to discourage house finches. Goldfinches can hang upside down to reach the seeds, whereas other birds cannot.

Other Food Notes

Apples

Apples attract bluebirds, chickadees, jays,

mockingbirds, robins, starlings, thrashers, titmice, towhees, and Carolina wrens. You can cut the apples in half or cube them. Don't overwork your presentation. Even small birds can feed on apple once the skin is broken. Put these fruits in suet feeders, in an open ground feeder, or add spikes to a piece of wood or an existing feeder to hold the fruit halves in place as birds feed.

Bacon Grease

Bacon grease attracts all sorts of birds and other animals as well. If you like, you can try to attract bluebirds, crows, jays, ravens, starlings, woodpeckers, and Carolina wrens with bacon grease presented in tuna cans or yoghurt cups. Some backyard bird feeders cap these

Ground-feeding birds, such as doves, quail, towhees, and sparrows, enjoy proso millet.

Apples, oranges, and other fruits can be mounted on special fruit feeders. Baltimore orioles and many other birds will eat fruit.

containers and freeze the grease until needed. Those frugal feeders can suspend a "container" by poking a wire through its edge and suspending it from a tree branch. This, of course, works best when temperatures are low, so that your grease stays where you put it.

Berries

Berries attract many different types of birds and are especially attractive when they're not available from natural sources. Savvy feeders freeze overripe berries during the summer for use in the winter.

When to Fill Feeders

Birds need food in every season. Winter storms provide an opportunity for you to brush off the snow and feed some hungry birds. Insects are dormant and tree sap is still.

Spring offers a time when insects and other food sources are not yet available, but birds are molting and preparing for the breeding season, so feeding is well appreciated during this time also.

In summer, birds are still feeding the year's hatch. Adult birds, feeding enormous amounts to their young, could use a helping hand through your feeder program.

In fall, migrants pass, refueling for the next part of their journey. What better time to feed hungry birds? Also in the fall, overwintering birds are recovering from the breeding season and will appreciate the extra calories.

Don't worry if you spend several weeks without feeding. Birds are not severely affected by switching to other food sources. Opportunists, birds locate the easiest source of food and use it. Typically, they will have little trouble locating another food source.

Regarding the time of day you fill your feeders, this depends on the traffic at your feeder and your habits. If you fill the feeders late in the day, you can see birds feeding as the last backyard activity before dark and the first in the morning without making a trip out too early.

However, if you have problems with other wildlife emptying your feeders in the night, and you wish to discourage this, feeding in the morning will help you get the results you want: feeding birds and not nocturnal visitors.

Feeder Placement

Placement of feeders makes all the difference to the birds and to your comfortable viewing. The perfect feeder types filled with the best seed will not attract birds if they are misplaced. Similarly, the perfectly placed feeder doesn't inspire you if it's difficult for you to see and difficult for you to get to, especially during the winter months.

Your view of the feeders, the presence of sheltering plants for quick cover, feeder height, prevailing wind, and ease of filling are important to satisfying results for you and your backyard birds. You can address all of this through feeder placement.

Viewing

Position your feeders according to how you spend time in your home. You can watch your birds from the kitchen window while washing dishes, from your kitchen table during breakfast, or from a more relaxed position in your family room. If you home-school, a perfect place is outside your classroom window. If you have a home office, try a feeder outside your office window.

Place your feeders so that it will be convenient to fill them even on cold winter days.

Prevailing Winds

Consider the direction of the wind you receive in the fall and in winter. The coldest air generally comes from the north. The best locations shield feeders from the wind, using either your home itself or a tree or outbuilding as a windscreen. Evergreens are excellent weather blockers, because they are effective in winter and summer. A feeder placed on the protected side of an evergreen is an attractive location: Feeding birds get a meal and a break from the elements. The evergreen also serves as cover.

Cover

You might think that because birds can fly, cover is not "a big deal." What you'd be overlooking is the instincts of a creature that survives because it is always scanning the skies and the ground for danger. If you consider the energy required to stay constantly alert, you'll have a better understanding of why cover is important to birds.

Birds are likely to consider even an unbelievable selection of tempting foods as too dangerous to approach if it is 30 feet (9 m) from cover. The likelihood that a hawk can swoop through, plucking them from the feeder, or that a cat can jump and grab them makes birds hesitate. Rightly so.

The same buffet of treats close to brush piles or thickets of bushes makes feeding at your station a safe choice. Once the bird disappears into the brush, it can "lose" its pursuer.

One last point relative to predators: The maximum height most house cats can jump is 5 feet (1.5 m) The maximum leap for most squirrels is 10 feet (3 m) from the nearest branch. These distances may help you fine-tune your feeder placement.

Pets and Feeders

Pets are lured by the prospect of food. Feeders offer seed, suet, and other foods to dogs, as well as the fun of frightening the birds away in a dramatic rise. For cats, the allure is all about hunting. Bells on cats, just like bells on dogs, do nothing to help birds.

What helps birds is restricting pets from feeder areas and providing cover that allows the birds to feel safe. If you have a backyard for your dog, restrict him from that part of the yard where the feeders are located. If you have a cat, keep her indoors.

Neighbors' pets can cause problems, too. Motion detector devices that shower water on unwelcome pet visitors are available from most garden supply stores.

Convenient Maintenance

Many people make feeder placement decisions during good weather. Feeders that seem conveniently located during June seem impossibly difficult to traipse out to in February, through snow and ice. If you have to shovel snow to reach your feeder to fill it, how often will you do this? If you have drifts, consider a window feeder that you can refill from inside.

To create your best option, imagine your yard during the worst weather you have. Now reconsider your placement.

If you can open the back door, take the seed from a shed, and fill the feeder without taking many more steps, aren't you more likely to keep the feeder full? If you and your kids can see this feeder from your kitchen or den window, are you more likely to notice what goes on there?

Water Experiments

Water, especially the sound of moving water, is more of an attractant for many birds than food. In an arid climate, water is scarce. In a northern winter, finding open water for bathing and drinking is difficult. When you have a consistent source of water in these circumstances, the birds will find you.

Even temperate-climate backyard bird enthusiasts swear the water wins out over the food every time. Many different types of systems work. The

Filling the bird bath is a great chore to give to a child who enjoys backyard birds.

fun is in finding which works best for you and your backyard flock.

Seasonal Thoughts

On warm, dry days, water evaporates quickly. On cold days, water freezes rapidly. Handy people can create water sources that automatically refill. Some clever people create birdbaths that use electricity or solar power to keep the water flowing instead of icing over. If extremes are not an issue, the traditional birdbath on a pedestal, with an inch of water in the bowl, is a good, all-around solution.

If you're not a handy person, many catalogs, online sources, and local bird stores include birdbaths that will solve weather problems.

Start simply. If you face Minnesota winters, consult your local bird-feeding store for a solution that works in your area and in your specific situation.

FAMILY-FRIENDLY TIP

Parents Helping Kids

Activities for parents, in addition to Project FeederWatch, include classes at your local Audubon chapter or at your local bird-feeding specialty stores or local parks and recreation districts.

Do-it-yourself parents and their kids can build a variety of birdhouses, roosting boxes, and feeders from plans available in special books available from your local bookstore or library. At the library, check the section classified under the Dewey Decimal number 639.

Home-schooling parents can use Project FeederWatch as a part of their program. For information about how to do this, reference http://www.bsceoc.org/national/pfwguide.html.

Sometimes the simplest solution is not a complicated device but excellent local advice.

Birdbath

As you discovered in Chapter 1, the simplest water system is a shallow dish placed on a post or deck railing. If the bottom of the dish is slippery, use pebbles to provide a firm footing for your birds. A more complicated arrangement is to suspend the dish. Drill three equidistant holes in a shallow dish, insert S-hooks into the holes, attach a wire to each S-hook, and connect the wires to a single S-hook at the top. Place a screw eye in the location from which you wish to hang your dish. Use the S-hook to install your bath.

The same factors that govern feeder placement apply for a birdbath. You'll find maintenance simpler and more convenient if watering and feeding occur in the same area. A single trip takes you to the water and the food areas for cleaning and refilling. A single solution for below-the-feeder maintenance is less work and more enjoyment time for you.

Permanent Spray

Take advantage of an existing watering system to fill a shallow birdbath each day. Reroute one emitter, or, if you use broadcast spray system, place the bath where it will catch water and still provide some cover for your birds. Birds will also bathe in the leaves wet by regular sprayers.

Garden Watering Systems

When you design or update an automatic sprinkling system, keep your backyard birds in mind. If you have or will install a drip irrigation system, use one emitter that sprays, perhaps into your birdbath or onto a slightly concave rock. Birds can choose to bathe during the early morning watering or in the residual water later in the day.

Low, dense shrubbery that catches a significant amount of water from a broadcast watering system can be a favorite bathing site for birds in the early morning. Birds tend to bathe earlier in the day, so that they will be dry when they return to their roosts at night.

Small Ponds

Some people install water features to attract backyard birds. When the needs of birds are kept in mind, ponds can increase your backyard bird fun by attracting more birds and providing another range of behavior for you to observe. When the features are designed for the homeowner, they usually don't work well for the birds.

What birds need is shallow water and secure footing. If you intend to install a small backyard pond with recirculating water, for example, purchase a shallow plastic liner, and use rocks to "raise the floor" of a portion of the pond so that the birds can walk in to water of no more than an inch in depth. The use of rocks also gives birds a rough surface to stand on while they dampen their lower sides and push water over their backs, just as they prefer. Plants in the water feature provide cover and attract insects that most backyard birds enjoy.

Ponds that require birds to wade in more than an inch of water are too deep. A plastic bottom, slick with algae, prevents birds from having a secure footing. The result is a pond that works for fish but not for songbirds. Many people with ponds constructed this way may find herons and raccoons fishing on a regular basis.

Before installing a pond, give thought to its placement, just as you would a feeder. Seeing your pond from your regular indoor perches magnifies your pleasure.

Nest Experiments

Many backyard birders thoroughly enjoy watching birds pair up, build nests, and

Portable Drip

If you are a photographer, use a portable drip to bring birds into lighting and backgrounds for more artful pictures. The set-up materials are basic: a plastic water bottle or milk jug, a bit of wire, and a plate or pie tin. Using a penknife or nail, make a small hole in the base of the jug. Suspend the water-filled jug from a branch or other weight-bearing object. Place the pan or plate underneath. The water drips into the plate. Refill the jug from the pie tin using a funnel or a plastic bag. The sound attracts the birds.

Nest Box Dimensions

Precise entrance hole diameter is the key to keeping a nesting box exclusively for your intended species. Measure the box depth from the front of the box where it joins the roof to the floor. This table is adapted from Corkran's *Birds in Nest Boxes*.

Bird Species	Entrance hole diameter (in./cm)	Distance of hole from box bottom (in./cm)	Floor dimensions (in./cm)	Height of box from ground (ft/m)	Other notes
Bluebird	1.5/3.8	6/15.2	5 x 5/12.7 x 12.7	5-10/1.5-3	Place on fencepost in grassy sunlit area
Chickadee, Nuthatch	1 1/8/3.5	8/20	4 x 4/10 x 10	10-12/3-3.5 above ground preferred. Position in tree with a small branch about 6/2 m from opening	Fill box with wood shavings (not sawdust). Birds will excavate shavings to create nest bowl
Wren	1 1/8/3.5	8/20	3 x 3/7.5 x 7.5	5-10/1.5-3 above ground on building, tree, or post	Place in brushy area to provide plenty of cover
Swallow	1.5/3.8	8/20	4 x 4/10 x 10	At least 5/1.5, but prefers 10-12/3-3.5 above ground	Fencepost or freestanding pole, building or tree where no branches are anywhere near entrance
Downy Woodpecker	1.5/3.8	8/20	4 x 4/10 x 10	6-20/2-6 above the ground	Fill box with wood shavings (not sawdust). Birds will excavate shavings to create nest bowl.

rear young. Although some birds may not need your help, providing nest sites and materials can bring birds close enough for you to observe. Cavity-nesting birds definitely need our help. Providing additional appropriate sites for their nesting helps keep them competitive with our nonnative birds, which are aggressive competitors for the few available cavities.

Nest sites for birds include the ground, shrubs and trees, standing dead trees, and human structures such as ledges, eaves, and roof tiles. In addition, you can create nest sites that imitate those preferred by birds by building a "substitute" nesting site. Nest boxes or birdhouses are one important aspect of the nesting equation.

It is important that your next boxes open for easy cleaning.

Building Nest Boxes

Dimensions

The dimensions of a nest box are important. Each species needs a particular size nest hole, nesting cavity depth, and interior floor dimensions. The nest hole allows the bird to enter, but excludes larger birds and many other predators. The depth of the cavity is about providing a separation from the elements and space for the bird to build the nest within the box. Finally, some predators reach inside nest cavities. The depth of the box is the depth that the species selects to

prevent the stealing of nestlings or eggs.

Materials

If you use scrap wood to make your nest box, do not use wood treated with preservatives. Dried lumber, especially cedar or exterior plywood 3/4 inch (2 cm) thick is a material that will last.

Placement

Each species has box height placement requirements. In addition, when placing your box on a tree, remember that the tree will continue to grow. Rather than using nails that may pull loose as the tree grows in diameter, use a lag or hex bolt that you can loosen to keep your nest box in place.

Backyard Bird Activities

Modifications

Many traditional-looking bird houses include perches at the entrance hole. While the perches seem enticing, predator birds use them as platforms for nest robbing. If you purchase boxes, be aware that perches are not always a helpful feature.

Other Considerations

To select the types of birds to attract with nest sites, consider your region, your specific habitat within the region, and the location of your yard relative to features required by the bird. To start, refer to the profiles in Chapter 3. Observe those birds that naturally come to your yard. Start by providing a nest box, if you like, for one of those birds. Watch and learn.

Another important source of information on this topic is your local Audubon chapter. This group has many members who are knowledgeable about the birds in your area and willing to share their knowledge with others. Specialty bird-feeding stores in your area may, in addition to having advice for you in the store, have programs that bring experts to your backyard to help you design a feeder and nest box setup that will work for your specific requirements.

Depending on your habitat, nest boxes can attract birds to your yard that feeding alone cannot.

Eastern bluebirds rarely come to feeders; they are more likely to come to your yard for a proper next box.

Keeping Records

Each person records her bird experiences differently. As you connect with other backyard bird enthusiasts, you'll learn more about what others do. Frequently used methods include a journal and various kinds of lists.

Journals

A journal entry is a description of what mattered to you about what you saw. You might keep a journal of what you see at the chair where you drink tea on Saturday afternoons. Perhaps your journal is something you write in at night, recounting your gratitudes of the day. You can add pictures, quotes, and even a list, if you like.

Field journals are available that have waterproof paper and sturdy bindings. A journal you'll use at your chair-side table can be a 99-cent notebook or a beautifully leather-bound book. The point of the journal is to take pleasure in making your entries and to take equal pleasure in rereading your notes days, months, or years later.

If you have a talent for sketching, or even if you don't, you might enjoy trying to capture a body posture, even using stick figures, to remind yourself of what you saw.

Special occasions for keeping notes include the building of nests and rearing of young, as well as the installation of new feeders and your observations about the types of birds that come to them. Keeping a journal does not exclude keeping lists.

Lists

Keeping bird lists takes many forms. Some types of lists frequently kept include daily, weekly, monthly, and annual lists of the birds that visit your yard. You can either jot the birds down in the order you see them or put together a checklist with columns to check off birds as you see them.

Such lists tell you the date of arrival of certain birds so that you can see the pattern of birds arriving and leaving each year. Migration schedules, surprisingly, deviate only a day or two in arrival dates from year to year. Monthly calendars tell you whom to expect, and you'll love the anticipation. Some families keep these lists on their refrigerator or near the window where family members watch the feeders.

Other types of lists include birds that fly over the yard but do not stop at your feeders. For example, sandhill cranes and bald eagles frequently fly over some Pacific Northwest and California yards. Those lucky families keep lists of those nonfeeder birds.

You can compare your lists with those of other backyard bird-watchers that you meet through your

How to Record a Sighting

Some people enjoy reading through recordings made during the year. You can do this either in a notebook that looks more like what a scientist would keep or one that's more like a scrapbook or memory book. You can make recordings daily or when you see something that's especially interesting to you, or both.

Make a note about the weather and the approximate time. Which birds came to the feeder or were involved in the behavior? What did they do? What was especially interesting about it? Was there anything unusual about the plumage? If you made a sketch or took a photograph, tape it in the book.

Other ideas: Use marker pens in bright colors when a new bird appears. When there's nothing happening at the feeder, reread your journal to remind you of your favorite experiences.

local Audubon Society chapter. Many of those members will have lists of their own, and the chapter leaders will be glad to put you in touch with people who have interests similar to yours.

A backyard bird feeder will become interesting to other regional birders when a rare bird consistently visits that feeder. Local bird groups often ask permission of homeowners to bring a few people to see the unusual bird. Many backyard bird feeders develop long-lasting friendships with people who share their interest in birds.

Project FeederWatch

You can turn your observations into science by participating in Project FeederWatch. Backyard bird enthusiasts from all over North America participate in leading scientists' projects by collecting data from their own backyards.

For 20 years, Project FeederWatch volunteers have collected bird count data, describing the changing distribution of birds across North America. Our list of the top 50 North American feeder birds is based Project FeederWatch data from 2006.

You can join Project FeederWatch and provide data from your feeders. Participants receive a newsletter and instructions on collecting information. Sharing your information with scientists and citizens interested in birds worldwide is a great way to double your fun. The small cost for participating in the program supports bird-related research.

For example, information you provide can help scientists compile data about interactions between predators and birds, or track the spread of house finch eye disease.

Learning More

No matter what aspect of birds fascinates you, there's a group that shares your fascination. From counting birds to painting them, more than 50 million North Americans focus leisure time on birds. The Resources section at the end of this book has dozens of ideas for you to learn more, network with others, and otherwise get the most out of feeding backyard birds.

How to Find Local Organizations

The best way to find local organizations concerning birds is through the National Audubon Society. One of their local chapters can connect you with people, bird-feeding suppliers, and local educational resources, whether classroom, field trip, informal, or online. You'll also learn about sister organizations through your local chapter. Contact the National Audubon Society at www.audubon.org/states/index.php or by telephone (212) 979-3000.

FAMILY-FRIENDLY TIP
Activities for Kids

Bird-oriented activities for kids depend on their ages. Kids can make observations and create pictures of the birds that appear in their backyards either by drawing or photographing with a digital camera.

Kids can also observe birds in other parts of the country through "feeder cams." One excellent feeder cam is at the Cornell Laboratory of Ornithology (www.birds.cornell.edu/pfw/News/feederCam/index.html).

"The Big Sit" is an activity you can do alone, or as a part of a regional activity, often sponsored by your local Audubon Society chapter. Take a day or the better part of a day and watch your feeders, recording the birds you see. At day's end, if you are participating in a larger group activity, report your feeder information. If you've done this on your own, add your list to your collection of other lists. One rainy day, you'll enjoy recalling your "Big Sit."

Much data about birds come from the activities of volunteers, like yourself, who enjoy sitting and watching what goes on around you.

The following are some surprising things you might see while just sitting.

Birds Forming a Giant Ball

Birds will show you where their predators are. Watch birds rise from the feeder, for example. Starlings rise in "balls," tightly formed clumps of birds that fly back and forth, maintaining this ball shape. For starlings to behave this way is a sure sign that an aerial predator is near. The ball moves to keep the predator below and to track his movements.

Dissimilar Birds Feeding Together

Birds of different species feeding together form what are called mixed flocks. Examples include downy woodpeckers feeding with black-capped chickadees. The chickadees are more alert to danger. Birds that eat a similar diet find more good food sources when they feed together.

Birds Cocking Their Head to One Side

Robins and other ground-feeding birds cock their heads to one side so that they can hear insects and worms better by pointing an ear toward the sound. Birds also cock their heads to see better. A bird's eyes don't move, and their ears don't have an "external sound collector." These head movements allow birds to use their senses better.

Birds Throwing Away Seeds Without Eating Them

Some birds throw away two or three seeds for each one they eat. When birds grab food with their bills, they evaluate whether the food is the right size. If the food is a seed, they determine whether they can crack the shell. Cardinals are poor at opening soft and small seeds, so they drop them. Thin-billed pine siskins drop large seeds and look for small ones they can open.

Chapter 6

Advanced

Backyard Birding

Challenges arise in every pastime, and backyard bird activities are no exception. You'll encounter problems with a pet or wildlife. You'll become obsessed with attracting a particular type of bird that doesn't visit your feeder. Birds will show behaviors you don't understand. A baby bird will call pitifully from across the lawn. This chapter helps you solve these common problems.

Problem Solving

The key to solving problems with bird feeders is to realize that they all have to do with food and natural behaviors. The challenge is that your natural instincts have little to do with how an animal sees the situation. The primary focus of pets, wild birds, and other wild animals is on food and safety. You can solve many problems using this knowledge. Most solutions lie in "putting the food out of reach."

Roaming Domestic Animals

Cats and dogs must be unable to reach feeders. The best solution, if you have a cat, is to keep it indoors. Bells make no difference, because cats stalk without making the bell sound. In addition, most birds do not respond to the sound of a bell. The American Bird Conservancy estimates that three-quarters of a billion birds are killed each year by roaming pet and feral cats. Place feeders where birds can detect cats approaching. Elevate feeders 5 feet (1.5 m) or more, which is outside the jump range of most cats.

Dogs usually harass birds and knock seed to the ground. Most dogs will eat seed, given the opportunity. This plays havoc with their digestive systems. Birds will not come to a feeder that they perceive to be unsafe. Finding a way to keep pets away from feeders is part of the process of feeder positioning.

If the cats and dogs that approach the feeder are not yours, discourage them by using sprays of water, fences, and aversion tactics.

Wildlife

When food is used as a lure, any wildlife that can possibly use that food also appears at your feeder. Wild animals are blind to the consequences of being undesirable to humans and will repeatedly visit the site of your bird feeders.

Although some backyard bird feeders love whatever animal happens by to sample the bird chow, other people experience great frustration and

Keep cats and other pets indoors to prevent them from hunting the birds you are trying to attract.

sometimes loathing of the animals that appear. The cast of other wildlife characters that often appears at feeders includes hawks, squirrels, opossums, raccoons, skunk, voles, mice, and rats. Some of the same tactics that work for roaming domestic animals also work with raccoons.

Hawks

Hawks are not a problem in the natural world. They are simply a part of that world, and a necessary part. Hawks do kill other birds as a part of their diet. The reactions of backyard bird feeders range from delight at seeing the aerobatics of Cooper's or sharp-shinned hawks at their feeders to guilt for attracting birds to be killed.

The solution to this negative view is to realize that you are not causing songbirds to be killed by attracting them to your feeder. Rather, you are causing them to be killed in a location where you can see this event. Hawks are birds coming to feeders, not to eat seed, but to eat other birds. Those hawks will kill other songbirds, if not the ones at your feeder. It's how they live.

Bully Birds

Jays and mockingbirds can be feeder bullies. Jays tend to intimidate other birds, so you might consider adding a feeder surrounded by a wire cage that excludes jays and other larger birds.

Getting Help With Problems

In this fastest-growing sport (or pastime or obsession) in North America, getting help is as easy as asking for it. The sources most available to you are:

- Your backyard bird-feeding store
- Your local Audubon chapter
- Your local parks and recreation department
- Your favorite listserv or website

People love to share their knowledge. As relieved as you may be to receive an answer to a problem, the person you ask will be as delighted to be able to help someone solve her problem.

If you're unsure how to contact these resources, check the Resources section.

Mockingbirds often make a very specific effort to eliminate other birds from the feeder. This happens because they decide that the feeder you thought was yours is actually theirs. They pursue birds that cross into their territory. They may also pursue you when you attempt to service the feeder.

Sometimes, after a couple of weeks, the mockingbird gives up defending the feeder. Sometimes not. An approach that often satisfies both the mockingbird and you is to move the feeder to a different location. An alternative is adding a second feeder in a different area, out of sight of the mockingbird.

Nuisance Birds

If you're not excited about house finches, house sparrows, rock pigeons, and starlings, minimize their impact by taking advantage of their feeding preferences. Pigeons and house sparrows would rather eat cracked corn than sunflower or Nyjer thistle seed. Fill one feeder, a decoy, with a less expensive seed where they can eat their preferred diet. Starlings can be "decoyed" to a table feeder where apple cores or moist dog kibble will keep them busy.

Weight-sensitive bird feeders that close when a heavy, nuisance bird steps onto the perch may also be helpful. The lightweight, preferred birds perch and feed with no problem. When the nuisance arrives on the perch, his weight closes the feeder opening.

A third option is to exclude birds over a certain size. You may have seen feeders surrounded by wire cages. The wire mesh is large enough to admit the "target" species but too small to admit the nuisance species you're attempting to exclude.

Your local nature stores can help you learn how to exclude birds common to your area. As an example, this trick works for starlings, who are real food hogs, especially at the suet feeder. Starlings have weak feet. Use this shortcoming by excluding them from the feeder top with a dome that forces birds to cling to the side. Although starlings will get some suet, clinging to the side wears on their weak feet. Starlings will drop to the ground before getting much.

Squirrels and Raccoons

Food gluttons, including mammals, can frustrate backyard bird feeders through decimating supplies of expensive seed or the last of the suet supply. Know that squirrels and raccoons often steal suet secured to trees. To prevent this, place the suet in metal wire feeders and suspend the feeder from a wire.

Another way to exclude squirrels and raccoons is to use baffles. Metal is the best material, because squirrels or raccoons cannot chew through metal as readily as they can plastic. Pole-mounted feeders need a baffle between ground and feeder. To deter squirrels, the tube baffle must be 14 inches (35.5 cm) long. To deter raccoons, it must be 24 inches (61 cm) long. You can install PVC pipe over the pole and spray-paint it for a less obtrusive tube baffle. For hanging feeders, install a baffle between the hanging hook and the feeder.

Some authorities suggest using capsaicin, the chemical that makes the "hot" in hot pepper, as a deterrent for squirrels. Squirrels, unless their circumstances are desperate, will not eat capsaicin-treated seeds. The concern of other authorities is that birds do not normally encounter capsaicin in their diets. Most biologists hesitate to recommend anything that is outside the naturally occurring songbird diet. In addition, your pets and children can accidentally grab hot pepper-laced seed.

An alternative solution is to provide a squirrel decoy. Squirrels prefer corn. Cracked or cob corn for a corn feeder is less expensive than seed and typically draws squirrels away from your prize seed.

Two popular types of squirrel baffles are the cone baffle (right) and the tube baffle (left).

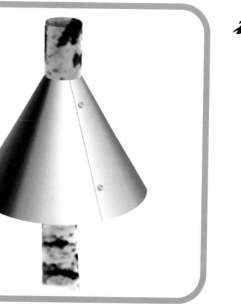

By the way, flying squirrels are nocturnal and interesting animals to see. Leave the seed out at night and your outside lights on to see them.

Ants

Ants can be a problem at feeders containing fruit or nectar. An effective deterrent is the ant guard. These guards provide water wells, barriers the ants won't cross, or a bell shape that ants do not navigate. Another layer of deterrent is petroleum jelly on the feeder itself or on the inside top of the guard. Products with glues that catch and hold work on hummingbirds as well as ants, so stay away from those products.

Rats

Norway rats are attracted to stored seed and the waste that falls below your feeder. Metal cans keep your seed (mostly) protected from the rats. Take care to sweep up seed spills to avoid attracting them to the area of the cans. High-quality seed reduces waste below the feeder. Also, raking below the feeders keeps rodent attractants to a minimum.

Opossums

Opossums are North America's only marsupials. Opossums have long gray fur except on their naked feet, ears, and tail. When opossums discover a feeding station, they become a frequent visitor, eating just about anything. Nocturnal feeders, these mammals are active throughout the year.

One approach to defeating nocturnal mammals is to put seed out in the morning and supply an amount adequate for the day. In this way, little is in the feeder to attract wandering night mammals. A second approach is to use a small radio or other device that transmits the sound of the human voice. Opossums, in particular, seem to avoid the sound of people's voices. Do be careful not to disturb your neighbors.

Feeder Debris

The area under the feeder can become unsightly with debris of uneaten seed and seed hulls. You can eliminate debris under your feeders by purchasing hulled seed. Hulled black-oil sunflower seeds, peanut pieces, and suet are

Field Guides

Many field guides to wild birds are available. Here are two to get you started:

Robbins, C. S., Bruun, B., & Zim, H. S. (2001). *Birds of North America: A Guide to Field Identification*. New York: St. Martin's Press.

National Geographic Society (1987) *Field Guide to Birds of North America, 3rd Ed*. Washington, DC, National Geographic Society

This feeder has a screen to prevent squirrels from eating the seed, but it still allows this pinon jay to feed.

examples of no-mess foods. All the seed is eaten, and birds have no "lower-valued" seed to sweep aside. In addition, no hulls drop to the ground. This limits the attraction of your under-feeder area to roaming scavengers.

To keep your under-feeder areas even neater, use a 3-inch (7.5 cm) layer of wood chips below the feeder. Whenever the area seems a bit messy, turn over the chips to disguise hulls and cover bird droppings.

One note about sunflower seed hulls important to gardeners: Sunflower seed hulls contain a chemical that retards germination and growth. Hulls can create problems for plants and especially seeds you want to sprout beneath the feeder.

Landscaping for Your Birds

Landscaping for birds creates a better habitat than you can achieve with feeders alone. Layering gives a habitat richness. Groundcovers and low-growing annuals and perennials provide cover and some nest sites. They also harbor insects that are food for your birds.

Shrubs and moderate-height perennials give another layer, attractive to those birds that feed off the ground. Vines and small trees provide another. Large trees or snags provide a top layer. Because you provide these layers, a greater number and variety of birds come to the yard.

The same principles apply whether you have 2 acres or 20 square feet (1.8 m^2). Flowers, small trees, vines, shrubs, groundcovers, even seasonal color baskets provide nest sites and cover.

In your yard or patio, provide plants that offer seed, berries, and fruit to your backyard birds. Select some plants to support nectar-feeding insects that draw birds that eat them.

The most effective landscaping to attract birds uses a mix of trees, shrubs, and flowers.

Native plants often are best attractors of birds that live in your local area. When you have a choice, native plant use has many advantages. Native plants are well adapted to your soil and climate. This means that the maintenance is far lower and plants grow with less effort than if you use exotic plants. Neighborhood garden centers and nature stores can help you with information about what native plants attract birds in your local area.

The idea of "benign neglect" is one approach to gardening for wildlife that takes some experienced gardeners by surprise. Leave the understory plants and dead flowers standing during the winter. Their seeds provide winter food. Leave your brush piles rather than disposing of them. These areas give birds a great place to hide and even nest.

How to Start

Food, water, cover, and nesting sites are the essential elements to keep in mind when landscaping for birds.

Evaluate Your Space

Try to look at your area, whether patio, large acreage, or small yard, from the bird's perspective.

What features do you have that are attractive to birds? Do you have trees

Backyard Education Programs

Educational programs about landscaping to attract birds are available through county extension programs, local college adult learning programs, and nurseries around the country. Some local Audubon chapters sponsor programs on "birdscaping."

and plants that are special favorites of birds? Plan to keep those features.

In landscaping, layering is important. Think tall, medium height, and low, and a mixture of densities. What shrubs are helpful? Which ones do birds never touch? Think through this at each existing layer.

Now, what would you like to add? Food? More cover? A water feature? The principles apply no matter the size of your space.

Visit Local Nature Stores and Nurseries

Nature stores often use native plants for landscaping. These stores also integrate feeders, landscape plants, and water features, so that you can see how these elements work together. Nurseries that carry native plants also often create nature-friendly displays. These displays are helpful in learning about the plants that grow well in your area, and that have attributes attractive to your birds.

Plant Selection

Among the plants you see at your nursery or in references, some will be good choices if you want to provide food for your backyard birds. Others are more functional as shelter or cover. Others may be ideal for nesting. To select plants that help meet your expectations, think about which of these aspects is most important to you. Add those plants first.

Food

To provide food for birds, think not only of the type of food, but the season in which the food will be available. Here are some choices to consider:

Early berries: Serviceberry, chokecherry, and honeysuckle

Midsummer berries: Blackberries, raspberries, blueberries, currants, gooseberries, elderberries, salmonberries, thimbleberries, and wineberries

Fall berries: Dogwood, viburnum (except Southwest)

Winter berries: Barberries, sumacs, roses, hollies, pyracantha

Vines: Honeysuckle, grapes, Virginia creeper

Sunflowers attract many seed-eating birds, such as house finches.

Fruit: Cherry, hackberry, juniper, red cedar, mulberry
Seed: Maple, box elder, pine, spruce, oak

Shelter

Shrubs: Juniper, rhododendron
Vines: Grapes
Trees: Juniper, pine, spruce

Nesting

Shrubs: Alders, elderberries, lilacs, roses, and willows
Cavities: Aspens, cottonwoods, oaks, and sycamores

Flowers

Use annual flowers in landscaping, on your patios, or in window boxes.

Tickseed sunflower, a self-sowing plant, is nice for a sunny hillside. It has masses of tall fragrant yellow flowers that attract chickadees, finches, redpolls, and sparrows.

Tall cosmos in red, pink, or white attract finches. Annual sunflowers are a tall single-stemmed flower that, planted at 2-week intervals, provides a steady seed supply for your birds.

Impatiens works well on patios and other shady borders. This familiar plant attracts hummingbirds, as well as cardinals and grosbeaks.

Marigolds are excellent box flowers, ruffled in gold, rust, or maroon. These attract juncos and native sparrows. Zinnias are also fast-blooming favorites in every color that attract cardinals,

chickadees, goldfinches, redpolls, siskins, sparrows, and titmice.

Perennials have the advantage of self-care, allowing you to concentrate on other aspects of the garden. Purple coneflowers self-sow, attracting finches, juncos, sparrows, and towhees.

Liriopes produce short, grassy clumps with white or purple flower spikes. The black berries that develop later attract mockingbirds. Goldenrods attract goldfinches and sparrows. Try combining with blue or purple late-blooming asters.

Ideas for the Terrace, Patio, or Balcony

In small spaces, creativity in using the space you have is key. That, and rigorous selection of the birds most likely to visit your area. You need to eliminate, at least in your initial plan, birds that are less likely to visit. Accommodate those you love most.

If you live in an apartment building, the building association may have rules regarding feeding of birds and plantings on the balconies. With artful planning, you can satisfy your love of birds and the building regulations.

Vines growing on trellises can provide seed heads and foliage for windbreaks and cover. Espaliered fruit trees or berry-producing plants can provide a winter of foraging and use little space.

Hanging baskets for the spring can also add useful plant material without using "floor space."

A variety of plants will attract a variety of birds (and butterflies).

continuous sound that adds interest for you and your bird friends.

A nest box or shelf in your mini-habitat could be the home of your favorite local bird resident. If you provide water, food, and cover, birds will come. Don't forget to add a feeder or two to your mini-garden.

Attracting Target Birds

If you've used the simple setup described in Chapter 2, the single feeder and water source, you've experienced the range of birds that visit your backyard. You recognize the ones you like to see and the ones of less interest to you.

Using the profiles and photographs in Chapter 3, you should be able to name most of them. The next step is to make a list of your favorite visitors and your least favorites and draw up your plan. For example, if you would like to attract goldfinches and exclude squirrels, look for the food that attracts the goldfinches (Nyjer thistle) and look for ways to limit squirrels' access to your other feeders. One solution includes baffles above and below the feeder.

Trees work on ground level terraces and patios. Consider trees carefully if your outdoor space is a balcony; in particular you may need to estimate the weight of damp soil and plant material.

Containers, including low boxes, terra cotta pots, and window boxes for balcony railings, are all ways of adding layers to your small space garden.

Birds will come to water, even if you're on a balcony. A small recirculating fountain produces

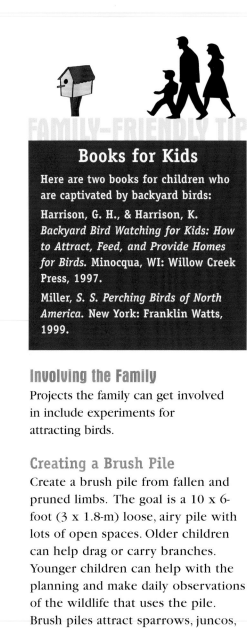

Stringing a Bird Planter Wire

Fun for kids to watch the progress. String a clothesline between two trees or posts, at least 10 feet (3 m) long and 6 feet (1.8 m) high. As birds perch on the wire, droppings fall below. Seeds excreted into droppings grow into berry-producing plants the birds like.

Investigating Dead Trees

Let the dead tree stand. Kids can investigate, looking for insects that use the bark and lay eggs there. Beetles bore into the wood. Woodpeckers may excavate nest holes.

Reusing Your Christmas Tree

Stand your Christmas tree a short distance from your feeders. Watch what happens. Do you get more feeder birds? Kids can take notes or just watch. Your kids can even decorate the tree with edible bird treats such as berries, peanut butter and seed-covered pine cones, and plain popcorn.

Injured Birds

Calls to wildlife rehabilitation centers spike in the spring and summer, when people call about baby birds that have fallen from nests. Generally, if the bird has some feathering, this is a part of a natural process called fledging. Most songbirds leave the nest before they can fly. The parents bring food as the baby bird moves about the yard trying out his wings and his hopping skills.

FAMILY-FRIENDLY TIP

Books for Kids

Here are two books for children who are captivated by backyard birds:

Harrison, G. H., & Harrison, K. *Backyard Bird Watching for Kids: How to Attract, Feed, and Provide Homes for Birds.* Minocqua, WI: Willow Creek Press, 1997.

Miller, S. S. *Perching Birds of North America.* New York: Franklin Watts, 1999.

Involving the Family

Projects the family can get involved in include experiments for attracting birds.

Creating a Brush Pile

Create a brush pile from fallen and pruned limbs. The goal is a 10 x 6-foot (3 x 1.8-m) loose, airy pile with lots of open spaces. Older children can help drag or carry branches. Younger children can help with the planning and make daily observations of the wildlife that uses the pile. Brush piles attract sparrows, juncos, wrens, chickadees, and tufted titmice. If they live in your area, quail will also use a brush pile.

The best help you can provide is to leave the bird alone and keep your cat indoors.

Naked birds fallen from the nest are likely not to survive. The best chance the bird has is to be returned to the nest. If you can't find the nest, tack a small box on the tree trunk where near where you found the bird and put the bird inside. If the bird can call at all, his parents will attempt to feed and keep him warm.

Glass Strikes

One hundred million to 1 billion birds each year are killed in the United States by striking glass. Birds try to fly through the glass, thinking it is clear air. Sometimes, reflections of the sky in the glass confuses them. When they strike the glass, they usually die.

If you find a bird that has struck glass, the best thing to do is to move the bird to a shady location with cover. If the bird was stunned, he'll recover and fly away.

To reduce bird strikes, add awnings, beads, fabric strips, or stickers to your windows.

In placing feeders, keep in mind that feeders placed near windows eliminate harmful strikes at that window. The bird is focused on the feeder and not flying "through" the window to the other side.

Disease Concerns

The news is full of scary information about birds and disease including West Nile virus and avian flu.

Letting dead trees stand in your yard provides nesting and foraging places for many birds, including hairy woodpeckers.

Although these diseases are a concern, feeder birds are not the problem. As with all disease, we must look at how the disease is spread and use that information for prevention.

Disease Spread Bird to Bird

In bird populations, a small number of birds carry disease. Sometimes, through direct contact and other times through fecal material, bird-to-bird infection is accelerated where many birds are concentrated. Periodic cleaning with the bleach-water solution helps keep feeders disease free.

If you see sick or dead birds around the feeder, take that opportunity to empty, clean, wash thoroughly, and disinfect your feeders. Disinfecting solution is 1 part bleach to 9 parts water.

Apply and let dry for 15 minutes. Rinse with fresh water and dry.

Carried by Mosquitoes

Mosquitoes transmit West Nile virus to people, to birds, and to other animals, such as horses. The simplest prevention is to eliminate your exposure to mosquitoes.

Close your home to mosquitoes. Check and repair window and door screens. When your "perimeter is secure," keep screens closed, especially in warm weather.

Eliminate water, no matter how small the amount, that stands for the four or more days mosquito larvae need to hatch. Check flowerpots, pet bowls, buckets, and spa covers. Change the water in birdbaths daily, pouring out all the old water, and replacing it with fresh.

Dead Birds and Disease

If only one bird has died, then you have no idea whether the bird died of old age or a cat bite or head trauma from hitting a window, even if you see evidence of disease on the bird.

If you find several dead birds around your feeder, do two things. First, bury the carcasses of the dead birds to avoid more exposure. Second, be sure to empty and destroy the seed and to wash and disinfect the feeders before replacing a new supply of seed. You might consider moving the feeders to a different location in the yard if a convenient one is available.

Unless your "die-off" is remarkable in number, city, county, and state authorities are not interested in testing the carcasses, no matter how upsetting the bird death is to you. If you have several instances of numerous bird deaths occurring at your feeder, discuss this with your neighborhood association or with your State Fish and Wildlife Department.

Keeping your feeders clean will help prevent spreading disease from bird to bird.

Bird flu (H5N1 avian influenza) is spread through direct contact with an infected bird's saliva, nasal secretions, or droppings. Frightening newspaper accounts from various parts of the world tell about people becoming ill after handling sick birds.

This bird flu is difficult for people to catch. Here are some cautions to prevent that unlikely event. Cleaning your feeders regularly and washing your hands afterward is important. Avoid touching backyard birds with your bare hands. For an update on bird flu, check with the Center for Disease Control at www.cdc.gov/flu/avian/.

Resources

National Organizations

American Bird Conservancy
PO Box 249
The Plains, VA 20198
Phone: (540) 253-5780
Fax: (540) 253-5782
www.abcbirds.org
American Bird Conservancy is a not-for-profit organization whose mission is to conserve wild birds and their habitats throughout the Americas.

American Birding Association
4945 N. 30th St.
Suite 200
Colorado Springs, CO 80919
Phone: (800) 850-2473
Fax: (719) 578-1480
member@aba.org
www.americanbirding.org
The ABA represents a whole range of birding interests, from identification and education to listing and conservation. Focused on experienced birders.

Society of Canadian Ornithologists
Thérèse Beaudet
Secrétaire aux membres / SCO Membership Secretary
128, Chemin des Lièges
St-Jean de l'Île d'Orléans (QC)
Canada   G0A 3W0
Tel : (418) 829-0379
Fax: (418) 829-0584
beaudet.lamothe@sympatico.ca
Canada's ornithological community body, involved with awards, publications, and linking professional ornithological societies in Canada, North America, and worldwide.

National Audubon Society
700 Broadway
New York, NY 10003
Phone: (212) 979-3000
Fax: (212) 979-3188
www.audubon.org
A network of community-based nature centers and chapters, scientific and educational programs, and advocacy on behalf of areas sustaining important bird populations that engages millions of people of all ages and backgrounds in positive conservation experiences.

National Wildlife Federation
11100 Wildlife Center Drive
Reston, VA 20190
Phone: (800) 822-9919
www.nwf.org
A great organization. In particular, consider their program to certify your backyard as a wildlife habitat. Fun, productive, and educational.

Magazines

BirdWatcher's Digest
P.O. Box 110
Marietta, OH 45750
Phone: (800) 879-2473
www.birdwatchersdigest.com/
An online and print publication focused on the interest of beginning and intermediate birdwatchers and feeders.

Wild Bird
P.O. Box 6040
Mission Viejo, CA 92690
Phone: (800) 365-4421
www.wildbirdmagazine.com/wb/home.aspx
A magazine that caters to beginning and intermediate birdwatchers and feeders.

Online Directories

Birdchat
//listserv.arizona.edu/cgi-bin/wa?A0=birdchat
National birding online cooperative, BirdChat provides a forum in which to share knowledge concerning wild birds. Lively discussions on topics related to wild birds, birding, and birders are invited to join.

Bird Links
www.nmnh.si.edu/BIRDNET/BIRDLINKS.html#birding.
Links to many local and national bird-related organizations.

Birding in Canada
www.web-nat.com/bic
A web site entry to Canada's birding resources.

National Bird Feeding Society
www.wildbird.com/content/nbs.index
Sponsored by the Wild Bird Centers, National Bird Feeding Society works to make backyard bird feeding and watching better—for people and the birds, by supporting education and research about backyard wild birds.

Peterson Online
www.Petersononline.com
Links to many sites on birds and other wildlife from the makers of the Peterson Field Guides.

Virtual Birder Online
www.virtualbirder.com
A portal to other online sites about birds that is convenient and easy to use.

Books

Bird Behavior References
Read, M. (2005). *Secret Lives of Common Birds: Enjoying Bird Behavior Through the Seasons.* Boston: Houghton Mifflin Co.

Sibley, D., Elphick, C., & Dunning, J. B. (2001). *The Sibley Guide to Bird Life & Behavior.* New York: Alfred A. Knopf.

Natural History Guides (a.k.a.Bird Lifestyle)
Ehrlich, P. R., Dobkin, D. S., & Wheye, D. (1988). *The Birder's Handbook: a Field Guide to the Natural History of North American Birds.* New York: Simon & Schuster.

Kaufman, K. (1996). *Lives of North American Birds.* Boston: Houghton Mifflin Co.

More on Bird Feeding
Roth, S. (2003). *The Backyard Bird Feeder's Bible: the A-to-Z Guide to Feeders, Seed Mixes, Projects, and Treats. Emmaus, PA: Rodale.*

More on Wildlife Gardening
Zickefoose, J. (2002). *Natural Gardening for Birds: Simple Ways to Create a Bird Haven.* Emmaus, PA: Rodale.

Resources

References

Corkran, C. C., & Labelle, B. A. (2004). *Birds in Nest Boxes: How to Help, Study, and Enjoy Birds When Snags Sre Scarce*. Happy Camp, CA: Naturegraph Publishers.

Dolezal, R. J. (2005). *Birds in Your Backyard: A Bird Lover's Guide to Creating a Garden Sanctuary*. Pleasantville, NY: Reader's Digest.

Dunne, P. (2003). *Pete Dunne on Bird Watching: The How-to, Where-to, and When-to of Birding*. Boston: Houghton Mifflin.

Ehrlich, P. R., Dobkin, D. S., & Wheye, D. (1988). *The Birder's Handbook: a Field Guide to the Natural History of North American Birds*. New York: Simon & Schuster.

Elving, P. (2000). *Attracting Birds*. Menlo Park, Calif: Sunset Books.

Furtman, M. (2004). *Why Birds Do That: Forty Distinctive Bird Behaviors Explained and Photographed*. Minocqua, WI: Willow Creek Press.

Hansen, Judie, and Mike Houck. (1991). *Wild in the City: A Complete Guide to Growing Your Own Wildlife Oasis.* DVD. Wild Hare Media.

Nehls, H. B., T. Aversa, & H. N. Opperman. (2004). *Birds of the Willamette Valley Region.* Olympia, WA: R. W. Morse.

Peterson, R. T. (1961). *A Field Guide to Western Birds.* 3rd ed. Boston: Houghton Mifflin.

Peterson, R. T. (1980). *A Field Guide to the Birds: A Completely New Guide to All the Birds of Eastern and Central North America*. 4th ed. Boston: Houghton Mifflin.

Podulka, S., R. W. Rohrbaugh, & R. Bonney. (2004). *Handbook of Bird Biology*. Ithaca, NY: Cornell Lab of Ornithology in association with Princeton University Press.

Rattigan, C. F. (Producer). (1989). *Birds of the Backyard*. DVD. Company for Home Entertainment.

Roth, S. (2000). *The Back Yard Bird Feeder's Bible.* Emmaus, PA: Rodale.

Sibley, D. (2002). *Sibley's Birding Basics.* New York: Alfred A. Knopf.

Stokes, D. W., & J. F. Lansdowne. (1979). *A Guide to the Behavior of Common Birds.* Boston: Little, Brown.

Stokes, D. W., & L. Q. Stokes. (1996). *Stokes Beginner's Guide to Birds.* Boston: Little, Brown.

Stokes, D. W., & L. Q. Stokes. (1998). *Stokes Bird Gardening Book: The Complete Guide to Creating a Bird-Friendly Habitat in Your Backyard*. Boston: Little, Brown.

Thompson, B. (1997). *Bird Watching for Dummies.* Foster City, CA: IDG Books Worldwide.

Wauer, R. H. (1999). *The American Robin.* Austin: University of Texas Press.

Index

107

108

111

Acknowledgments

The author wishes to give special thanks to David Bonter, Ph.D., Leader, Project FeederWatch, Cornell Lab of Ornithology, for providing data from Project FeederWatch for use in the selection of birds for inclusion of the book, reporting the ranges of these birds, and other assistance. Grateful thanks is owed to Steven Margolin, Elisabeth Magnus, and Suzy Williams for reading an early version of this manuscript. Errors and omissions are mine and not those of Project FeederWatch or my early manuscript readers. Finally, the author wishes to thank Tom Mazorlig of T.F.H. Publications for his generous editorial assistance.

About the Author

Carol Frischmann holds a B.S. in Science Education from Duke University and has pursued her passion for wild birds by serving as President of Mt. Diablo Audubon Society and by working in wildlife rehabilitation facilities for many years. Carol spends much of her time watching birds in her own backyard in Portland, Oregon, as well as across the United States, Central and South America, Australia, and Africa. Carol writes on pets and nature for magazines and newspapers and is the pet columnist for KGW.com, an NBC affiliate television station, and for her own website ThisWildLife.com.

Photo Credits

Ron Austing: 9 (bottom), 10, 31 (right), 33 (left), 34 (left), 35 (all), 36 (top left and right), 43, 45, 46 (left), 48 (bottom left and right), 49 (all), 50 (all), 51 (right), 76
Laurie Barr (courtesy of Shutterstock): 14
Suzanne Boehning: 93 (drawings)
Tony Campbell (courtesy of Shutterstock): 4, 40 (left)
Judy Crawford (courtesy of Shutterstock): 97
Derek Dammann (courtesy of iStockphoto): 26
Jeff Fishbein: 18, 29 (right), 30 (right), 38 (all), 68, 70
Ronnie Howard (courtesy of Shutterstock): 9 (top)
Raymond Kasprzak (courtesy of Shutterstock): 34 (right), 55
Kaytee Products, Inc.: 16,
Larry Kimball: 6, 8, (right), 37 (left), 40 (right), 44 (right)
Peter LaTourrette: 9 (center), 32 (left), 39 (left), 41 (left), 90
Bruce MacQueen (courtesy of Shutterstock): 33 (right)
Barbara Magnuson: 12, 23, 28, 30 (left), 42 (left), 46 (left 2nd column), 64, 65, 95
V. J. Matthews (courtesy of Shutterstock): 77
Martine Oger (courtesy of Shutterstock): 52
C. Paquin (courtesy of Shutterstock): 46 (right 2nd column)
Rafi Reyes: 19, 74, 75, 99, 103
Rob & Ann Simpson: 29 (left), 31 (left), 37 (right), 42 (right), 44 (left), 47 (left), 48 (top left), 51 (left), 60, 73, 84, 92,
Raymond C. Truelove (courtesy of Shutterstock): 24
John Tyson: 36 (bottom left), 39 (right), 47 (right), 56, 57, 62, 67, 79, 83, 88, 101
Maleta M. Walls: 71
Author photo courtesy of Absolute Images Fine Photography.
All other photos courtesy of T.F.H. archives.

REACH OUT. ACT. RESPOND.

Go to AnimalPlanet.com/ROAR and find out how you can be a voice for animals everywhere!